ROCK 'N ROLL WOMAN

ROCK 'N ROLL WOMAN

BY KATHERINE ORLOFF

Nash Publishing, Los Angeles

PHOTO CREDITS

Photo of Claudia Lennear courtesy of Warner Bros. Records.
Photo of Nicole Barclay courtesy of Warner Bros. Records.
Photo of Toni Brown and Terry Garthwaite [page 67] courtesy of Capitol Records.
Photo of Grace Slick [page 151] by Dennis Anderson.
Photo of Grace Slick [page 152] by Debbie Hurst.
Photos of Toni Brown courtesy of MCA Records.
Photos of Carly Simon courtesy of Elektra Records.

Library of Congress Catalog Card Number: 73-93974
International Standard Book Number: 0-8402-8077-7

Published simultaneously in the United States and Canada
by Nash Publishing Corporation, 9255 Sunset Boulevard
Los Angeles, California 90069

Printed in the United States of America

First Printing

CONTENTS

ROCK 'N ROLL WOMAN

INTRODUCTION

It is extremely difficult to be a woman in rock and roll. As Terry Garthwaite says, "Rock and roll is set up for men," which leaves women little to do but fight an uphill battle, both for audience acceptance and for their own sense of worth. Off stage, women's roles seem well-defined with lines sharply drawn and duties specific, but on stage, certain areas become clouded, and few people seem certain of where priorities lie and what the boundaries are. The purpose of this book is to explore the feelings and the life-styles of women who make their living in rock and roll, on-stage in front of bands, and on records. They are committed to their music, have no alternative choices, no careers they would rather consider. The woman's movement has helped them become more aware of themselves and more aware of the reasons for their frustrations. The music business and the people concerned with profit and loss have often helped underline the female performer's position of inferiority.

What people nebulously refer to as "rock and roll" incorporates three distinctly separate areas. There is a tremendous difference between the music, the music business, and the life-style itself. In addition to its purely musical aspects, the music also encompasses a means of communication, performer to audience. For many performers and musicians it is the way in which they best relate to other people. Each of the interviews in this book left me with a good feeling of having been able to unearth important emotions. But the question still exists: If the music doesn't say it, how can feelings be explained in words? What I am interested in, then, is attitudes and approaches to music, and interpretations of experience. The music has a life in and of itself.

The music business is another matter. Like any other enterprise motivated by competition and income, it is run by numbers, by sales figures. Performers hear discussions about units and product and royalties and contracts. It is significant that the better schooled, financially aware performers are the ones who most rarely drown in their own mismanagement. This type of acumen is usually foreign to many women who have traditionally come to accept that business and finance are men's functions. Even though there are untold numbers of male performers who have been cheated in the recording industry, women are still thought of as being more vulnerable. Often this is their own fault because they encourage the image.

The business end of rock and roll exerts a tremendous amount of pressure on musicians to produce. Contracts usually call for a prescribed number of albums per year, whether or not the material is of top quality. In addition, rock people are, to a degree, at the mercy of promotion men whose job it is to get records played on the radio. Groups have become successful without AM radio play—Grand Funk Railroad is a prime example—but much depends on the amount of traveling and the number of concerts a group can handle. Few women have been able to get a break without precious radio play, and they have had to hope the promotion men consider them strong enough contenders to hold up against the competition.

It is the business element that is responsible for advertising and publicity and for meeting demands for recording studio time and equipment. In many cases, this has worked for musicians and not against them. When Wendy Waldman went on an extended road trip to promote her first album, Warner Bros. picked up much of the tab for her sidemen and made it possible for her to work her album, an absolute necessity for a new artist.

Aside from the record companies, rock and roll supports numerous related activities: private public relations companies, management firms, lawyers, accountants, booking agencies. These are distractions that tend to dilute a musician's energies. They are, however, matters that must be attended to. A musician's main concern is to make music, and he is fortunate to have people around who are trustworthy enough to see that everything else is taken care of. This is equally true in the case of a woman and raises the additional problem of authority.

The bottom line, however, is still having that contract, having a company willing to put records in the marketplace. As a rock and roll journalist, I would get numerous new albums every week and, after months of listening, I began to realize how very few were worth serious consideration. I began to lose respect for record companies that flooded the stores with inferior albums and for those publicists who, with a straight face, would persistently promote individuals or groups who were, to be generous, terrible.

A recent article in *Forbes* magazine quotes an unnamed record company executive as saying that rock and roll is "music by the inept for the untutored." I feel this is a fairly accurate estimate and, inevitably, there is a good deal of mediocre music. Yet the dedicated musician is more concerned with quality music than with life-style or image. The object is to continue working, to grow and to produce, hoping sales match good intentions. Obviously, these are areas where there is the most contention with record companies. The companies have to be accountable to stockholders and boards of directors who only look at the numbers.

The most visible part of the rock and roll world is the life-style, its particular attitudes, inflections, and accoutrements. Musicians' slang has become part of the common vocabulary, with words like "gig" and "changes" continually popping up in totally nonmusical contexts.

Fans model their own lives on those of their favorite rock personalities, and many believe that the music is part of their generation, an important part of their entire existence. Although the most ardent supporters and participants in the rock life-style are a minority of American youth, the usual middle-class definition of what a teenager or young adult should be disappears under reports of hundreds of thousands of requests for concert tickets to see the Rolling Stones or Bob Dylan and The Band.

The rock life-style supports countless retail outlets. Clothing boutiques, head shops, and record stores have radios, tapes, or records playing rock music to make their customers feel more at home by creating a sense of studied hipness.

The style has become so commercial, it seems, partly because of the short distance between audience and stage. Vast numbers of local rock groups tune up nightly, practicing and playing small clubs, hoping for a break. The ones who have made it very often started the same way. Age differences are minimal and so, frequently, is the talent differential. Aspirants look at the stars and remark, "Hey, I can do that." Sometimes they are right.

An interesting statistic gleaned from a *Rolling Stone* readership survey indicated that 75 percent of the magazine's readers are men. This is intriguing, because it seems to say something regarding rock and roll's central and strongest fans. It also seems to represent an accurate reflection of the business aspect of the medium.

Rock stars are the only culture heroes for many adolescent Americans, offering areas of identification that, for the most part, were once supplied by the film industry. Today, many American movies have become slick and unfeeling, the subject matter heavy-handed and boring, the anti-heroes well-defined losers. Pop stars are in the spotlight. They are real, and they are winners.

Women have had a difficult time settling into all three areas of rock and roll. As far as their roles in performance, much of the frustration and satisfaction is revealed in the context of the following interviews. It is interesting to note that none of the people here is considered a superstar. And none play what is considered hard rock.

Hard rock, that music I classify by its high decibel level and enormous energy quotient, has been the province of men. It is blaring, aggressive, mean music, possibly reflective of mean times. Even when Janis Joplin was fronting Big Brother and the Holding Company and singing as hard as any woman in the medium has, she seemed vulnerable. Janis was aggressive, but she was never threatening. Janis was hurt.

Much of the attraction of rock and roll has been its dynamic force, the energy of the music and intensity of its performance. There has been an obvious phallic connection with instruments, and in many cases an almost direct confrontation with audiences.

In general, women have preferred to take a softer focus. Their rock is less intense, more sensitive, more articulate. It demands more from its listeners, and it hasn't had the recognition that the male approach has. It is more difficult for women to be accepted as serious musicians and group leaders, and it is hard for many male musicians to acquiesce to female leadership in the recording studio. Offhand, I know of no successful women record producers.

At first glance, women are ignored even historically. All through the '50s and '60s, musical memories seem to center on male artists: Chuck Berry, Elvis Presley, the Rolling Stones, the Beatles. Women are remembered later, the Shirelles, the Ronettes, the Crystals, the Supremes, ironically most of them in the rhythm and blues context. The only female name which comes to mind when recollecting the so-called "British invasion" of the mid-sixties is Marianne Faithful, and her image, whatever its truth, was always that of a gentle, feminine, soft-spoken lady.

Women have done fairly well in the business aspect of their careers, but it seems that the most influential are the most invisible. David Rubinson, manager of the Pointer

Sisters, told me that he knows of at least three major record companies that seem to be held together by women. "It seems that whenever I have to call to get royalty checks or have some problem solved, I always end up talking to a woman," says Rubinson. His attitude is one of respect.

Women are responsible for artist activities, royalty payments, and record mastering and pressing, all of which are crucial to the proper functioning of a record company.

In addition, it seems that the most effective press agents in rock and roll are women. Men own the agencies, but women do much of the work. Depending on the needs of those they work for, these publicists tend to fall into types: The Little Girl, who stays mostly in the office and is very quiet and efficient; The Good Time Lady, who pals around with her clients; and The Mother Hen, who serves in general as a comfort and adviser. This is not to detract from any of them. They are excellent publicists and good people. They are just not in charge.

There are a number of women writers and reviewers, most of whom have been on the scene for at least five years. It is interesting to note that when *Coast* magazine did a rundown of Los Angeles rock critics, none of those included were women. I am fortunate in that, at least to my knowledge, I have never been discriminated against professionally because I am a woman. In a couple of instances, male press agents said they had expected me to be "a little old lady in a flowered hat." I never took that personally.

One of the most aggravating aspects of being a young woman writer is that sometimes your motives are questioned. Rock and roll is a very sex-conscious field, and the assumption is occasionally made that female critics are just groupies with a different gimmick.

Groupies seem to me to be a very sad lot. All the groupies I have ever met appear lonely and unhappy, young girls trying desperately to get attention, acceptance, and some sort of feeling into their lives. Rock and roll means so much to them that sex becomes their medium of exchange, and the cost, most of the time, is their self-respect and dignity. Enthusiastic fans are a blessing, but the groupie mentality has taken this enthusiasm to its absurd end. The phenomenon seems unhealthy and certainly dispiriting. Interestingly enough, there are few male groupies, and those who do exist often attach themselves to male stars, for both their own desires and to get more attention from women, but not from women performers.

Women in the rock and roll life-style tend to fall prey to traditional role definitions, and in order to play the game, they sometimes tend to become "one of the boys," sacrificing much of their femininity and personal originality to go along with the crowd. There is pressure to conform, and women fight both their own instincts and their cultural roles.

The energy and force of rock and roll, the pressures of its life-style, and the emerging importance of women in the field, create a good deal of conflict. Frequently this is most apparent in large concerts where audience demands are high. This is strongly interrelated to the idea of rock and roll as a scene.

In July 1970, I remember going to a show featuring Pacific Gas & Flectric, Grand Funk Railroad, and Ten Years After. The arena, home of the Los Angeles Lakers, holds about 18,000 people. The sound company had been working for two days to set up a balanced, usable system that would complement the needs of the performers. The show opened with PG&E at a moderate energy level designed to be inoffensive. However, when

Grand Funk began their set, all hell broke loose. Sound engineers stood transfixed in front of their oscilloscopes watching clipped sine waves.

"See those flat lines at the top of the screen?" one of them hollered. "They're just about to blow up the whole system!" Breathlessly they ran from amplifier to amplifier trying to accommodate the input. The noise was terrifying.

At the same time, authority-crazed rent-a-cops started dragging kids out of the arena by the hair. People stoned on reds and wine were baiting the cops. Outside, gate crashers were showering rocks and bottles on the Inglewood police.

The road manager for Ten Years After, noticing the look of unbridled panic in my eyes, made a spot for me on stage behind one of the giant speaker banks. He told me that no matter what happened, I should stay put until the end of the show, and keep my backstage pass where the right people could see it. He'd obviously been through this before. I was in the safest place, and since the noise was going the other way, the quietest. The pandemonium was unreal. It was the last arena concert I went to.

At this level, audiences have gone beyond the ability to be critical. They give standing ovations for mediocre sets, a fact which makes many musicians contemptuous and cynical. Some performers tend to attract the downer crowds. On tour with Neil Young, Linda Ronstadt witnessed more than a few, she said, who "looked as if they had to be carried in on stretchers and propped up in their seats." She calls them "primal screamers," and says the only thing they respond to is decibels, and about the only thing they can do is roll back their eyes and howl, "Boogie!"

At times I begin to wonder how important the music is to people who can't digest it unless they are in some comatose state. Mob psychology seems to come into play when people do things in crowds they would not do alone. They become anonymous and impressionable followers, looking up to frequently narcissistic leaders. It's frightening.

In addition, it often seems that the music is incidental. The attraction may be for the audience situation itself, the gathering of what those people like to think of as a common mind. I remember being at a rock festival some years ago in Northridge, California, where two young boys, whom I guessed to be around thirteen or fourteen, approached me and a friend and asked us if we had any marijuana they could buy. I was surprised, both by their youth and the directness of their question. They didn't know us, we were wearing backstage passes which identified us as something other than just audience, and we could have been working for the police. At that time, undercover police seemed to be at every rock event. Didn't they think of that? "Oh," one of them replied. His eyes were about three shades of purple and his speech had an almost incoherant glaze. "Don't you think if you tried to bust us, all these beautiful people would help us out?" I looked over the indifferent crowd and told him that I doubted it. He seemed very bewildered.

Even though in many cases these elements are in the minority, just the fact of their existence keeps a lot of people away from concerts which feature top groups.

In January Maria Muldaur appeared at Los Angeles's elegant Dorothy Chandler Pavilion, opening a concert to Loggins and Messina. It's 1974, I was told, audiences have calmed down. After Maria's set was finished and the intermission lights came up, people on the balcony levels launched scores of paper airplanes made from the ripped up sheets of the program booklets. The floor level began to look like a refuse heap. A strong argument for staying home.

Some sociologist armed with funds from a well-meaning foundation would have a field day trying to figure it out. Unfortunately, this type of pseudoscientific research usually comes up with conclusions any hip fifteen-year-old has known for years. Some clown gets $15,000 to study the relationship between rock music and violence, takes one look at Altamont where a man was killed and concludes, yes, there is some relationship here....

I don't believe in trying to predict human behavior. However, it does seem that there is an important force in American popular culture taking shape around contemporary music.

It seems a shame that one of the influences at work here is that of drugs. It is a continual source of sadness to me to see the correlation between rock and roll and drugs. My initial attitude toward drugs was one of mild curiosity. Slowly I became irritated, and, finally, angry. The issue is complex and disheartening. I saw the excuses, the desire for escape, the pressure on people involved in tremendous competition. I also saw a lack of self-respect, insecurity in the midst of adulation, and a strange need for self-annihilation. The complications arose when I realized that many of the performers and musicians whom I admire most are heavy users. Emotions run the gamut, as do physical beings, from depressing to dangerous. All of the sorrow I feel about the existence of the music-drug relationship was summed up in the death of Janis Joplin. There is a sickness here, and one whose existence is too often denied.

The idea of rock and roll as a scene was exposed to me very directly in the years when I first began to write about it. In the mid to late '60s in Los Angeles, there was a group of people involved in various aspects of rock who became, in a certain sense, a family. We were all working toward the same goal: to spread the word about the music. As noted, a good number of these people were women, writers and publicists and record company assistants. We helped each other, enjoyed each other's company, and in the best cases, became friends. Occasionally people would switch jobs, but they seldom did anything really different, just got checks from another newspaper, record label, or public relations firm.

We were all writers, to a degree. Those who weren't writing for publications, were writing press releases to be printed in those publications. There were also performer biographies and canned features. One of my friends worked her way through graduate school writing these features. She was astonished at the number of staff writers for large newspapers who used the stories verbatim and put their own by-lines on them. It seems there were enough incompetent rock writers and reviewers to balance out the inarticulate performers.

During these years, the record and PR companies helped writers get by. Much of the time I was earning from $50 to $100 a week writing rock and roll copy. In those days, there were two or three press parties a week, to announce an album, a new company, introduce a new act, a special concert or TV show. Much of the time the main attraction at these events was the food, catered and served, and gratis.

Most interviews were done over lunch at good restaurants. Frankly, I used to prefer the lunch interview for several reasons. People tended to be more relaxed when they were eating. I could always break the ice by discussing the menu or the parking problem. The situation seemed far more natural than sitting in an office, usually some pre-fab cubicle with a plastic shag carpet that makes static. In addition, since I rarely took notes or used a tape recorder, I felt more comfortable in a more social surrounding. Also, I noticed that you can tell something about a person by the way he or she eats, by what is ordered and how it is attacked.

These lunch interviews were, for the most part, successful but impersonal. I made note of the fact that very few of the subjects were women.

The interviews done for this book are among the best I think I have ever done. Aside from the fact that the subject matter is important to me, the situations themselves were often very personal and very open. I was invited into women's homes, an offer which I greatly appreciated both for its honesty and the respect it showed.

As for the press parties and expensive luncheons, we rarely saw the people who paid the bills. Companies were financial giants and some remote accountant was no doubt tallying it all up somewhere else. My publicist friends signed the lunch tabs and sent them "upstairs." After a while, I discovered that artists are billed back for these expenses. In an indirect way then, they are paying for free editorial space.

The situation is complex, for the system is subtle. Free concerts, free meals, free travel, free records, free clothes. Advertising T-shirts became a familiar sight packed in with records mailed to reviewers. Publications do little to offset this. They rarely, if ever, allow for expenses. They also pay very low wages. Fortunately, good writers are notoriously independent. I have yet to know of a favorable review of a bad concert or record simply because it was free. Those reviews are usually the result of rotten critics. The crime is that most entertainment editors don't know enough about music to tell the difference. This obvious credibility gap may give rise to grave doubts about other sections of newspapers and magazines, affecting everything from politics to sports.

For the most part, writers tend to give space to acts they like. They want to interview musicians who impress them. Even with an initially favorable prejudice, disappointments have been evident. There are few who go out of their way to be condescending or bitchy. Those who do are rarely taken seriously. I had one experience that was a conscious attempt at "influence." I was offered a trip to Hawaii if I would review a two-group concert and favor one of the groups. The press agent who offered me the trip knew that I had written a major feature about this group earlier in the year, and that I didn't care for the second group on the bill. Kind words in print and all expenses would be paid. I still haven't been to Hawaii.

For the most part, rock people rarely court writers. They know where the buck stops. Many of them feel that print publicity doesn't make any difference as far as record sales are concerned. Their main interest is in the broadcast media, particularly radio program directors and disc jockeys. Many feel that all the stories in the world won't come near to doing what one "Pick to Click" will for sales. To a large degree, print publicity is ego food, and it is rock star ego that keeps these PR companies alive. Perhaps their most valuable function is to help new performers gain audience recognition. It is also their hardest job. Otherwise, the credit for success must go to record promotion men who somehow get songs on the air.

Conflict in rock and roll exists, too, in that while audience demands are high, and there is a definite scene surrounding the genre, a performer is only able to give so much. I was disappointed in many interviews when questions which I felt were honest and straightforward were met with "yes," "no," and "whaddaya mean?" I was most disillusioned when I discovered that people whose music represented them as sensitive and intelligent turned out to be vacant, irresponsible, and boring. Of course surprises worked the other way, too. The music remains the common denominator. Can we also expect gifted musicians to be articulate cultural spokesmen? I think not.

Many times fans become possessive and personally demanding, writing letters to their idols asking for advice, continued correspondence, and sometimes personal commitments. This situation is often harder on women than it is on men, not merely because women have to struggle harder for audience acceptance and critical acclaim, but because most women I have spoken with tend to react on a more personal level. An adulating audience can create equal amounts of pressure with its attention. A poised woman thus will frequently impart a degree of distance with her professionalism.

Which brings us to a definition of terms and an attempt to set up some boundaries. The easiest way out is to define rock and roll as any popular music with a heavily accented beat and steady rhythmic structure. However, there is music which we broadly refer to as rock which does not fit the definition. To me, rock and roll embodies that dynamism, that movement and flash which characterizes much popular contemporary sound. It can be loud or soft, played by individuals or groups, presented instrumentally or vocally or in combinations thereof.

As a result, the term Rock and Roll Woman is a contradiction. If rock demonstrates that very masculine power, a woman is at odds with the definition immediately. While she can play the notes and sing the tunes, all the elements that have influenced her upbringing and attitudes tell her she is in the wrong place. Ideally, we think of women in the genre as having their own identities, their own particular musical and personal interpretations. It is unwise and unfair to compare them to men, to expect them to behave and produce like men. They are part of the rock and roll family, the complementary colors, valid on their own. They should be judged according to their own standards and appreciated for their own uniqueness. Just as Orientals see the yin and the yang on equal terms, rock and roll has its facets. Women don't need special concessions or excuses. They need to stand firm, and be heard.

All the women in this book were chosen because of their commitment to their music, their dedication to rock as a life-style, and their desire to be considered on their own terms. Each is establishing herself, a star on the rise in her own right. A few have been associated with groups but have ventured out on their own—to have more control, assert themselves—so that their ideas may be given form.

My choices were admittedly intuitive. Some women whom I very much wanted to include were not accessible due to time and distance. In addition, I did not include country and western or rhythm and blues women. They have their own genre, and should be the subjects of their own books. I pointedly did not include those performers I call the "showgirls," the supperclub circuit, designer-gowned performers who are talented singers, but nonetheless not rock-and-roll women. Among them are Barbra Streisand, Liza Minelli, Cher Bono, Diana Ross, and Vikki Carr. There are also singers who are on the fringe of this group, less showy, but whose audience tends more toward middle of the road, easy listening pop: Helen Reddy, Anne Murray, Dusty Springfield are examples. Not here are predominently folk-oriented artists such as Joan Baez and Mimi Farina, Judy Collins and Sandy Denny, or the intensely personal work created by the likes of Dory Previn and Laura Nyro.

Three omissions need further explanation. They are Bette Midler, Joni Mitchell, and Carole King. To me, Bette Midler represents an extreme. I think she can be a fine singer, and I am in full favor of her desire for her audiences to enjoy themselves. What bothers me is the predominance of flash, the emphasis on costuming and attitude rather than on the music. It is these things that make her a theatrical personality, a novelty act, more than a serious part of the music world. Audiences tire of novelty, and unless her music grows and develops, Bette Midler will not be able to retain the popularity she has built.

It is difficult to believe that the Bette Midler on stage isn't a show, an act. For the most part, the women in this book are what you see on stage. Midler includes some rock classics in her repertoire, but her interpretations take them to a completely different level. Too much show and not enough soul.

Joni Mitchell, on the other hand, is one of the most personally exposed of popular artists. Growing out of the folk tradition, she has written songs that are so revealing of her life and love affairs, that often other people cannot sing them with any conviction. She has had publicized relationships with several top musicians, which has led some to call her, rather coldly, the ultimate supergroupie. For this reason she has avoided interviews, even in cases where she might have been able to clear the air and set her mind at ease. I find this all very distressing, for I feel that she is truly gifted, an awesome talent and a moving performer. But Joni Mitchell is defeating her own purposes, seeming to turn ever inward, dependent on her relationships, almost as if she were using her music as psychotherapy. Rock and roll women seem to be more out in the open, having to accept the fact that they are targets for the sniper fire of criticism and failure. Slowly they are beginning to see that this is one of the things that makes them strong.

The most blatant example of artist insulation is Carole King. It was years before the public knew or cared that she was part of the Goffin-King writing team that produced a number of vastly successful tunes of the '60s. She was sequestered in an office in New York's famous Brill Building turning out material for top stars of the era. When she finally became a performer and went out on the road with James Taylor, her personal success was assured. Her albums run to astronomical sales figures and the nature of her songs allows other singers to cover them with ease. As for Carole King, she has a strict "no-interview" policy, with no exceptions. Communications are filtered through her producer Lou Adler, who will gladly tell interested parties exactly how Ms. King feels about things. She leads a very private life, and now doesn't even do much performing. There will be some argument that she has worked long and hard and deserves her privacy, a fact I will not dispute. But Carole King is not a rock and roll woman. She is a housewife who writes songs.

My first job as a rock and roll journalist marked the beginning of a relationship with equal amounts of accident, circumstance, and disappointment. The best moments usually involved the discovery of new talent, seeing stunning performances, and hearing unexpectedly remarkable albums.

Working for various publications subsequently convinced me that my labors were justified by the pleasure that I took in the music. Good live music can transcend poor surroundings. When the music complements the moment and the musicians are precise and cohesive, when the songs are melodic with lyrics that are honest and well articulated, there are few occasions that are emotionally more satisfying to me. It is during these infrequent situations that I begin to think of popular music in terms of serious art.

Here, then, are the views of some women who have a few things to say about their lives and times. They are offered with affection, and the hope that those of you who read this book might take the time to listen to their music—so that these interviews might come to life.

PROLOGUE

A new act to promote. A good-looking singer with her first solo album. It has cost her record company over $40,000 to get it into the stores. The young executive sighs and stares at the floor.

"If she'd only go down on the promotion men, we'd sell a million records."

A rock and roll lady has her choices. Partly because there are so many men around: musicians, agents, managers, club owners, record producers and engineers, businessmen, disc jockeys, and radio-program directors. Rock and roll women are thought of as product.

A myth exists: Rock performers are accessible, free-thinking, free-loving, hard-living individuals who do not have traditional moral values. And there are some of the stereotypical ham-handed cigar-smoking promotion people who try to take advantage.

Sometimes this leads to the inevitable alternative: integrity or personal preference versus the music business's version of the casting couch. Overnight sensations rarely last long enough to figure it out. Others become fighters.

Being a woman in rock and roll is not easy. It is difficult in the spotlight as a performer, and it is hard in the studio as a session musician. A woman in music wants to be taken seriously, and she must prove herself.

The situation is getting better, women are being recognized as part of the industry—one of the reasons this book exists. There are more women recording, more gaining audience acceptance, more receiving critics' attention. There is sadness only when the life-style takes its toll. Rock and roll women have to get out on the road and work. They work hard, and they have to keep at it. The result can be that for all the sweat, they have earned the adoration of people with whom they have nothing in common but their loneliness. The first and final example is Janis Joplin.

NICOEL BARCLAY

Nicoel Barclay grew up in the Washington, D.C., and Virginia-Maryland area, where, in the early '60's, the prevailing musical style was rhythm and blues. A loner as a child, she recalls her early desire to be a musician, an ambition that seemed directly accessible to her. She spent a short time in college, at Washington University in St. Louis and at Maryland University, but gave up school to devote herself to a serious musical career. In spite of her obvious enthusiasm and growing musical ability, her parents encouraged her to stay in school under the traditional assumption that she should have something to fall back on. Their feeling was that musicians are basically unemployable except as musicians. Nickey herself admits now that if she couldn't find work as a musician, it would be difficult for her to take what she calls a straight job.

The way things look at present, it seems doubtful that Nickey Barclay will have to find outside work. A talented piano and organ player and sometime dabbler in guitar, she moved West from Washington and began to be known around Los Angeles as an accomplished session musician. She was courted by an established trio that needed a keyboard player, but her personal experience made her reluctant to commit herself. The group was Fanny and the three other members were women. Having never been exposed to other women musicians, especially in the almost exclusively male rhythm and blues context of the East Coast, Nickey was initially put off by Fanny's desire to include her. She went on the Joe Cocker Mad Dogs and Englishmen tour, and returned home following a hectic, but musically inspired road trip. At this time Fanny was still interested, and after some informal jamming Nickey joined the sisters June and Jean Millington, who played guitar and bass respectively, and drummer Alice de Buhr, and the four of them set about establishing the fact that women could, indeed, play rock and roll.

Producer Richard Perry, whose credits include Barbra Streisand, Carly Simon, and Tiny Tim, took Fanny into the studio and produced the groups' first three albums, including *Fanny, Charity Ball,* and *Fanny Hill.* Todd Rundgren took over production of the fourth album, *Mother's Pride* before internal problems started plaguing the group.

As things worked out, June Millington and Alice de Buhr left the group in 1973 and were replaced by guitarist Patti Quatro and drummer Brie Brandt. Nickey feels the group is now better than ever, closer personally as well as musically. As for Nickey herself, she is intensely determined to make the group a lasting success.

Disillusioned by a failing love affair, she has turned her energies toward the group effort. Thoughts of becoming a solo act have been put aside, for she feels that Fanny is a reference point for women's bands and, as such, has a responsibility to persevere and to prosper.

Nicoel Barclay has mellowed quite a bit since the early days of her association with Fanny. Her unblinking enthusiasm still exists, along with her drive and an insatiable need to work. But there are moments of reflective quiet now, a more philosophical tone underlying her outlook. Still, these elements are more obvious on a personal level than they are on a musical one. On stage she is animated and energetic, singing much of Fanny's material, a large part of which she has written herself. Her voice has a bluesy raspy quality, which contrasts with her compact body and curly, close-cropped strawberry blonde head of hair.

It is indicative of the attitude toward female musicians that Fanny was thought of initially as a gimmick. Nickey's own scepticism about joining the group proves the point. They have been criticized because of the feeling that they have never reached their potential on record, but their live performances repeatedly have received rave reviews. Fanny is not the only group that is appreciated more after having been seen, yet it is one of the few groups that is taken seriously only when professional competence is physically displayed. Having established themselves as capable performers, the time has come, Nickey Barclay feels, to start using Fanny's collective sexual identity as a complement to the music. The assumption remains that an all-girl band, recognized as a polished musical entity, can effectively embellish its material with a feminine stage presence. Nickey Barclay thinks the time is right, preparing Fanny for another logical and consecutive step forward.

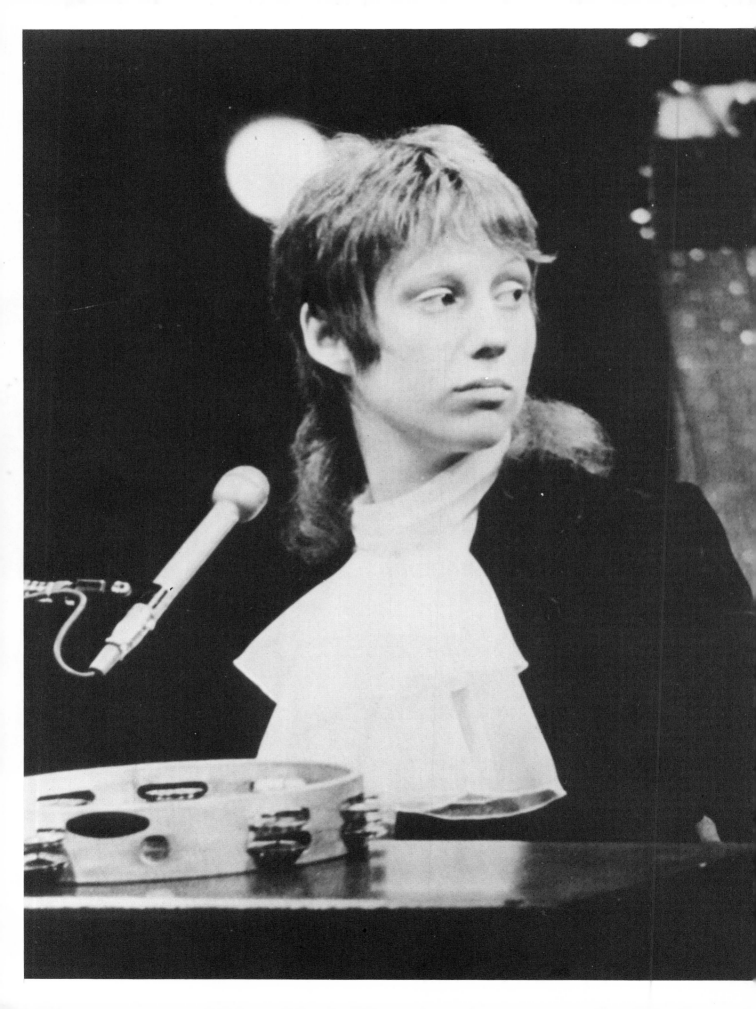

I always wanted to be a rock musician. I grew up with the radio. Ever since I was a little kid, my big brother had the radio on. I really got into piano players because, for one thing, my mother was playing a lot of jazz records, people like George Shearing. It's only been in the last year that that influence is starting to show. I must have filed all that when I was a kid. I'm starting to feel jazz, things that must have been in me all these years but locked away. From that I really started to listen to piano in rock records, like the Jerry Lee Lewis style. I decided when I was a kid that I wanted to be a piano player in a rock and roll band.

How did you
reach the decision to become
a rock and roll singer?

It never occurred to me that I couldn't. I was alone most of the time when I was a kid. I was good in school and I wrote poetry, and I liked to be by myself. So I had a hard time finding friends. About the only real friends I had were diplomats' kids and exchange students because they were more into literature and things like that. So I was always kind of alone and I did what I wanted to do in a lot of ways. It's kind of funny looking back at it, because it really never occurred to me, until people starting putting the question to us in Fanny, that I couldn't do it.

I was really into athletics when I was a kid. I was a real runt. I was short for my age and scrawny and pasty because I was always off in the woods. I was doing things that boys did at that age. This is what I've looked back on and tried to figure out because people have asked us this all the time.

I've also been singing all my life. No one in my family is in any kind of music, but my mother and my grandmother always used to

Did you think
you could actually do it?

sing. Whenever my grandmother came to visit, we'd learn things in harmony. So I was singing since I was very young.

When I was twelve, I just sort of suddenly discovered the world. I'd been pacing in my room for the whole summer, and I guess I reached puberty. I started with my first band, and I started going out with guys, and I started dope all at the same time. When I was twelve, I was about two years ahead in school and I was with older kids already.

I started out with a blues band. I was the singer, and there was a drummer, piano player, guitar player, and a sax player. No bass in those days. We just did local gigs. That same year I bought myself a guitar with money I made doing odd jobs, and learned to play it. I kind of divided my time between doing the folk clubs and singing blues, and being with an electric band. I saw both sides of it. I didn't play piano then. I was a stand-up singer, and I was in a lot of soul bands, because coming from the Maryland-Virginia area, that was the kind of music you did. It was me and a guy singer and a horn section. Sometimes there would be an organ player. The boys always wore leather coats and baggy pants, greaser gear, and I wore high heels, the cocktail bit. At this time I wasn't even playing guitar. That was something I did on the side.

I started seriously learning the piano when the Beatles' album *Sgt. Pepper* came out. I got turned on by an idea I had for a piano arrangement for "Fixing a Hole." So I sat down and learned it.

When did you start playing piano with a band?

I can't really remember when I made the transition to playing piano with a group. I think it was in the summer of '67 or '68, and I was in a group that did vocal harmonies. There was a guy on electric piano and I started showing him some chord progressions to some song we wanted to learn. After that I started doing a couple of numbers with the band. Then eventually I got into playing piano with groups and I drifted out to Los Angeles and started working in bar bands and doing cheap recording sessions for $25 a shot.

I couldn't afford to join the union in those days. I was working with a lot of groups in the Topanga Canyon area. There are a lot of would-be entrepreneurs in that area. It's one of those things. You play in bars and some manager will hear you and ask you to make a tape. I ran across guys who said, oh we'll take you in to make a demo, then you meet an engineer or somebody who'll help you get sessions.

How did you get together with Fanny?

In January 1970 Fanny already existed and was recording. They were looking for a keyboard player, and they had been signed to

Warners for about ten months. They spent thousands of dollars of their advance money flying girls in from all over the country trying to find somebody.

I was signed with a new thing that a guy I knew started called Musicians' Contact Service. You'd pay a couple of dollars and he'd give you a mimeographed sheet to fill out saying what you were looking for, what you played, what your influences were, what kind of equipment you had.

Fanny called me up through that service. They called me several times over a period of about three months, but I wasn't interested. I had never heard of another girl musician. They came from a whole background of girl bands. There was a big movement in San Francisco where they got together. Where I'd come from, I'd never even met another girl musician. There were hardly even any girl singers in most of the soul bands in that area. When I look back on it, I was actually something of an oddity, because all the girls were in the folk clubs.

You don't think about it until people start asking you. I guess that made me weird because I was just doing it, and quite often I was the organizer of the group, the leader. I was frustrated because I was writing and the caliber of the musicians at the time wasn't up to the writing. So I guess I was already unusual. Of course, I always used to get attention. It was much easier being the girl singer because your band protects you. I guess they figured then that girls had to be looked after. I did very well. I was never fucked over personally when I was singing with groups, even with my first bands. I was just a member of the group. I was just blind, is what it was.

I knew what I wanted to do, and I knew that I was a good singer and that I could perform very well. I'd been standing up with a microphone for years and years. When you're in a soul band, you have to perform, the show is 50 percent of what you're doing. The music is almost secondary. It's the show and the beat, and how you sing over it.

So I had this thing about showmanship, and I was just doing what I wanted to do. It's funny, because nobody ever told me I sang "good for a girl."

Finally, I was really broke and Fanny told me I could get session pay if I worked with them. So I went down to check them out, figuring I could make some money. They were very excited about the way I played, they really liked it. But I was put off. I guess I was spoiled. I was used to being the only girl in the group and that makes you unique, and I didn't have to think about being compared to other chicks on any level, whether it was singing or looks or dress or performance. They say that they never felt anything, but I felt paranoid.

I came back to the house after meeting them and I was in tears. Here were three chicks who really seemed confident at the time.

They were singing and they looked good and they were moving together. They seemed to have a real friendship and an understanding like bands have, but I'd never seen that with girls. They had to get back in touch with me, because I didn't call them. They said I was the best piano player they had found and they wanted me to join them.

I started doing sessions and helping them out with gigs so that everybody could pay the rent because they were really broke then. Then, through a friend—our drummer's sister, who was business managing the group then—we met the members of The Band. They had come to LA to do a concert. Rick Danko and Richard Manuel and their road manager came to our house for dinner. We all jammed after dinner and they liked our music very much. It was just one of those things. They tried to get us on the bill at a concert they were doing the following week in Long Beach, but they couldn't work it out. It was a really flattering offer.

After that Long Beach concert, we went to a party where there were a lot of music people, one of whom was Leon Russell. Rick, I think it was Rick, I'm not sure because we were all drunk, stood up and told everyone about these "amazing girl musicians" he had met, and he introduced everybody. From that Leon called up and wanted to use us on a session, and I used to go out to his house a lot and jam. One time when I was there, Joe Cocker and Chris Stainton were there and we played for a long time, and the next thing we knew, they were talking about getting a band together.

After one night of playing for hours and hours, Chris Stainton's girl friend and I started talking, and she began apologizing to me because none of the guys had complimented me on my playing. She said she really chewed them out because none of the guys had said anything, and, since I was a girl, they should have said something. I just looked at her, I couldn't believe what she was saying. The way I had seen it, without thinking, I had just gone over to jam and met some great people who I admired and wanted to work with for several years. It didn't occur to me that there was anything strange about it.

From your association with Leon Russell, you were included in the Mad Dogs and Englishmen tour. Was it hard on you?

Yes, I think it was hard on everyone. I was one of the few who came out of it in one piece. I got sick and had to drop out for a while and then join up again towards the end of the tour. I would never do anything like that again, but I'm glad I did it. It was mismanaged and disorganized. There were too many people.

After the tour was over I was sick for a couple of months. Then I was just back to doing to the same old thing, looking for gigs and session work. Fanny hadn't found a piano player yet. I had kind of run out on them because I didn't like their music, their influences. I had left them high and dry, just run off with about a week's notice and joined Mad Dogs. So there was a bit of wariness. But then somehow we got together. We started jamming and it just sort of grew. Without anybody talking about me formally joining, we went through the summer and played a lot of bar gigs together. All of a sudden toward the end of the summer we kind of looked at each other and said, hey, we're a group.

I think, at first most people thought we were "pretty good for girls," because they had never seen anything like us. They had no reference point. Now Fanny *is* the reference point. No matter what we do from now on, we were the first women's group to get international notice. Now when you see articles about new girl bands forming, they always compare them to us or mention us.

How do you think people reacted to Fanny initially?

I think we got away with a lot because we were girls, but at the same time, people were ten times as critical. I think all of our albums, for whatever flaws that they might have, have material on them which, if they had been done by a guys' group as writing or performance, would have gotten a lot more notice. I think people will go back to them and pick up on them, once they have completely accepted the idea of the group.

Once I had accepted the idea of a group of women, then it was just there. I came up through the same music traditions the rest of the guys have. You get attitudes, a band is a band. You think about the music. You don't get personal. Once I'd thrown in my lot, my head was spinning—recording contracts, real management. It was a big thrill. It was the first time any of that had happened to me.

We didn't. That's just now beginning. It matured the same way the group did. When we first started performing, we just went on stage wearing whatever we were wearing. We were clean and that would be about it. Looking back on it, I guess we must have been aware of image so much that we didn't think about it. I can see in the way we played and the way we lived and the things we did, that we did feel the pressure of having to prove ourselves. Play as much as we could, be as flashy as we could, and step on each other's toes. I'm sure that we really felt it. Because of that, for the first year or so we went through the phase of saying, "We're musicians, and then we're girls."

How did you determine what the group's physical image would be?

It amounted to us apologizing for being women, shying away from any kind of glamour or attractiveness on stage. We felt that Jean and June and Alice had gone through that with their other bands, matching skirts and pearls. They felt it was a symbol of more frivolous days. Then they moved to LA and got in with the dope-smoking, I'm-a-musician, that's-my-religion kind of thing, and they went funky.

Nicoel Barclay / 23

Do you feel pressure to be "one of the guys?" Do you think you have to be that way to be accepted by male musicians?

Well, it depends on what you call being one of the guys. Every once in a while, people will lay it on us that we are playing male music. The only reason that's true is that because up until now it was always made by men. Were playing rock and roll. People would ask us if we were playing hard and loud because we feel we have to be like guys to be accepted. We're playing hard and loud because we are four musicians who like rock and roll and that's the band we're in.

We never tried to be one of the guys on the road or in that context. At first we always wore jeans, but only because we wanted people to think we were serious musicians and not frivolous. I would say it would have been easier for us if we were men. There's no way around it. But then that's meaningless because we're *not* men.

Right now we're about to go back into the studio with our new guitar player and our new drummer. We were in a state of change for a long time. The biggest thing that we see now about being the first group of our kind is that in most groups of guys, if somebody isn't cutting it, there's an entire talent pool out there to draw from. If you need a lead guitar player, there are fifty lead players who will answer your audition call.

We stuck together because we all had a concept, but more than that, we stuck together because there was no place else we could get people. June was wrong for what the group is becoming despite her talent, but what could we do? She was a good lead player most of the time and she wrote a lot of our material. You just don't send out a call. How many girl lead guitar players are there in the country? We just had to wait. That meant that in a lot of ways, we're stronger. It was like being married and not being able to walk out. We went through emotional and business shit that would have broken up any male group, or any group that had a free pool of talent to choose from. As a result, there are an awful lot of scars on all of us inside, but we also know each other and the business better. All the quitters have quit now, and the people in this band are married to it now, as much as any musician has to be in this business.

Do women tell you that Fanny has inspired them to pursue music seriously?

Yes, we get a lot of mail like that, and girls come up to us and tell us that they would never have started playing if they hadn't heard us or seen us. That's part of the reward, but it's also part of the responsibility. It meant that no matter what we were going through we also couldn't break up, for that reason. We'd gotten to the point that we were well known enough, we had gone far enough that if we had broken up along the way, it probably would have been all over. People would have said, see, girls can't do it. There had been so much time and money poured into us. It was not hype, a lot of that money we never saw, but because we existed it was spent. We couldn't let people down.

24 / Nicoel Barclay

That's really scary. Not only do you know that you are stuck with the job, but you have to keep getting better and you have to really do it because you have people looking up to you.

I think that every business in the world is lonely, and that rock and roll is one of the professions that involves living and moving in a way that forces you to see that you're lonely.

Do you think rock and roll is a lonely business?

If you have a secretarial job and you're married and you've got kids, and you have a husband and a home and relatives and people down the street you play cards with, you don't realize it. You have all the trappings. In this business, you don't have the trappings around you. There's all the glamour and all those things people want, but that's when you start finding out that whether it's in business or in love, you can't trust anybody.

We used to say anyone who we get involved with has to understand that we're musicians, and what that means. I've been married and my marriage deteriorated because I'm a "creative artist" as a category, meaning someone who's always unhappy and who has to do something about it and write. That means that I'm very schizoid. If I flip into a working state of mind, it's like changing a gear. Theres no room for an emotional attachment, one that makes demands, because I have to be completely selfish, put all my energy into what I'm doing, into that music, that state of mind. When I flip back out of it, I'm just like any other woman, and I need a man. The problem is that a guy who isn't a musician can't understand that, and a guy who is a musician goes through it too, so there's no way out.

How does this affect your personal life?

I didn't used to think about it, but now I'm beginning to feel like a Woman In The Music Business. Now I'm beginning to feel like a freak. I've never had a stand on any political thing about women, the whole women's movement, because I've always been convinced that boys and girls are different in a lot of essential ways. At the same time, I've been just as deeply convinced, if not more so, that one does what one wants to do for a living. It just never occurred to me that girls can't do this or that. I just can't see it that way. In other words, nobody could ever stop me from being a musician, because that's what I want to do.

Only when I wasn't on stage. That's the reason I'm a performer. Anybody who's a performer is looking for love. It's that simple. You're looking for an ego boost because you don't feel you deserve it on a real-life level, I think. So I guess that's why I'm a performer.

Did you ever have any confidence problems?

Nicoel Barclay / 25

I've never felt any lack of confidence in my performing, I'll never understand how I could reconcile myself, my attitudes, because I believed so little in myself in every other part of my life, and yet when I went near a stage, it wasn't even a question of hamming it up, I always knew when I walked on stage that I was a queen.

Why, after so many years of confidence and actual experience, should you now feel so much like an oddity?

In the past few years, I've done a lot of growing up. I've learned what it feels like to be a woman and not be ashamed of it, which I had been all my life, not relating to music. I never felt like I could make the grade as a chick, which is weird because of what I was doing. Ever since I was twelve, I was always involved with a lot of guys, and that should have made me feel good, but it didn't. I always felt like I was putting somebody on. I always felt like somebody was going to catch me. Then I went through the ultimate fairy tale and got caught. From what I learned, I can see that it wasn't my fault, and I don't feel shattered by it.

I had been together for a long time with another musician. It really was a fairy tale. Two musicians meet on the road and discover that they hit it off together off stage. Where he came from, women are women, second class. He had so much masculine pride. He started making me aware of what it was like to be dominated for the first time in my life at a home level, but when it came to any kind of music, he was at my feet just like I was at his. If we ever started to have a hassle, we could pick up a guitar and solve it in a second. But by doing what he did, he made me feel like a woman. I don't care if that's sacrilege to the movement. He made me feel like a woman in every way, which is something that I'd never trusted anyone enough to allow to happen. But it couldn't have lasted, because like I said, we were too changeable.

In the end, he made me wonder if it's possible to be a musician, a pop star, and be a real woman who a guy would want forever, someone to have his children. As he pointed out, I'm married to music just the way he is, and I'm married in a way that you can't just walk out.

Now I want to do it all the way. I really want to make it big. Now it's sort of revenge almost, but not on any man, just on the way things are. I want to be able to show people. Because if I can't find fulfillment just as a woman, then I might as well go all the way and become a nun in terms of music.

It's like what happens when someone beats you running in track at school, and you decide you're going to cream him. You're going to turn into the best distance runner that the school has ever seen, you're going to show that fucker. Well, I figure that in the process of doing just that, you become so busy training, and so much into digging the running, and so much into being good at it, that it no longer becomes necessary to show that fucker.

I'm bound and determined not to lose. That has nothing to do with men or anything, because it's that thing about loneliness. You have to face yourself. That's one thing about creative people, you have to live with yourself, which a lot of people manage to avoid doing most of their lives. That's why we all die early in this profession, among other things. That applies also to actors and playwrights, but it's worse in music because the life-style is harder and the duration of what you are doing is so much less in most cases.

If I'm still alive now, after what I've seen about myself, after what people have shown me, after what I've done to people through being a musician, who loved me no matter who they were, if I can still live with myself, then I'm not going to knuckle under now or later. I want to somehow get past that. I figure I'll always be lonely, but there's got to be some way to make it a little easier.

It depends on where I am and who I'm with. I have no friends in the United States, except now my band, which I didn't even have before. When I'm in England and I'm with my friends, I play all the time. I go around to clubs, I'm with people. I only get over there once in a while, but then I live as much as I can because I know it won't last.

Do you hang out a lot?
Go to clubs and listen to other bands?

That's something else I've learned. Nothing is permanent, good or bad, when you're living this kind of life. I really think that musicians and performers and people like us live so much faster, just the mood changes I go through are amazing. You come off the road and after a week, it seems as though you've been home for a month. You're stir crazy.

Yes, and I don't like it. I don't feel as though people are open, in a way that I can relate to, which is funny because most people say that English kids are reserved. America makes it really easy to feel isolated. People don't fucking care in England. That country's been around a long time, and people don't care what you're like. I've never felt at home here.

Do you feel pressure to be cool here?
To act kind of aloof?

I saw myself there, and the same kind of self-destructive things that motivated her, and the fact that she died looking for love. She went all the way to the top. She was a myth.

You mentioned that you
were reading Janis Joplin's biography,
"Buried Alive." How did you react to it?

Nicoel Barclay / 27

*Do you really believe
that being a pop star and being
fulfilled as a woman
are mutually exclusive?*

I pray that they're not. But I can't tell right now. I'm in a state of real confusion. But I do know that there is only one thing in the world that I want more than to have children, and that's to be a rock and roll musician for as many years as I want to. That's number one, but number two is always there. I've had affairs and I've been married and nothing has affected me this way because I never really wanted to have a family.

*Do you think
of family in terms of being stationary,
having a house in the suburbs?*

I never grew up with stationwagons and dishwashers and all that. My mother was a schoolteacher and my father was a store clerk, so we didn't have much money. I didn't watch TV when I was a kid. I just read and wrote and I was alone a lot. I've got my own dream, a very private place with a lot of green. I hope that's still left when I can afford it.

*How have male fans reacted to Fanny?
Do you have any male groupies?.*

When we first started out, there wasn't much attention. People really didn't know what to think of us. Maybe at first they were a little threatened. But now it's amazing. There are all these pretty young boys with glitter on their eyelids who want to fuck us. They just follow us around. It's such a weird feeling to take a guy back to your hotel with you. It's so absurd and outrageous. But it's so much fun!

TONI BROWN

Toni Brown is a woman who is not afraid to speak her mind. She has spent time and thought formulating ideas and opinions which she offers openly on request. No equivocation, no hedging, no fence-sitting; you know exactly where she stands, both personally and musically. Her writing displays the same forthright qualities, and it is her writing that is most important to Toni Brown. While many other women in popular music are concerned with perpetuating their recording, performing, and, specifically, their singing identities, Toni wants to be known primarily as a writer. Now thirty-five, her goal is to be able to minimize the other elements of her career and to concentrate on the one. She has been building toward that goal for some time now.

Born in New England, Toni's childhood musical preferences influenced her own later styles. She was particularly fond of country and western music and listened frequently to Jimmie Rogers, Hank Williams, and Kitty Wells on Boston's country-oriented radio stations. Her first musical pleasure was singing and, soon after, she learned guitar to accompany herself. Nine years of classical piano training supplied the technical skill she needed to adapt to the folk idiom, and the keyboard became her preferred instrument.

Toni began writing songs in her preteen years, centering on the typical country and western format of unrequited love. The tradition provided what she lacked in experience. A more serious focus followed during her college years, when she studied creative writing and literature at Bennington College in Vermont, an exclusive, and at that time, women's school specializing in the arts. She earned her Bachelor of Arts degree after having spent her years there writing poetry and short stories.

While in college, her interest in music grew and she continued to sing and play guitar and piano with friends. Her musical tastes widened as well, to include jazz, gospel, rock, classical, pop, and ethnic folk music.

Since poetry was one of Toni's main interests at Bennington, she was naturally intrigued by reports of the Beat poets and San Francisco's "subterranean" culture. She came to the West Coast in 1960, but ended up across the bay in Berkeley in the midst of its burgeoning folk scene. There, Toni found a group of people who shared her musical roots and tastes, and with these friends she formed a country string band called the Crabgrassers, which played around the Berkeley area until 1967, when she met Terry Garthwaite.

Toni and Terry had known about each other for years but had never met. After they were introduced by a mutual friend, they decided to try to put together an electric band built around Terry's vocals and guitar and Toni's keyboards and harmonies; they both contributed original songs, and that band, the Joy of Cooking, became one of the most original to come out of the San Francisco Bay area.

With the Joy of Cooking, Toni recorded three ablums for Capitol Records, *Joy of Cooking*, *Closer to the Ground*, and *Castles*. She left the group in September 1972, after the strain of touring finally got to her, although she continued to contribute new songs to the group's repertoire.

Shortly thereafter, Toni and Terry went to Nashville to record an album of original country tunes. Titled *Cross-Country*, the album had been in the works for nearly two years. It received very favorable reviews, but only enjoyed limited sales. In a sense, it is still to be discovered. A problem may be inherent in its nature since it's not truly a country album per se, nor is it really rock, but rather more of a middle of the road, easy to listen to collection of good songs, well presented. In that very competitive area, being good is no longer a criterion for success.

In 1973 Toni signed with MCA Records, and her first solo album, *Good For You, Too*, was released in early 1974. Again, critics have acclaimed Toni Brown a writer of exceptional depth and talent, and placed her above several more popular singers, ones who can more readily be identified as personalities.

Toni Brown is fighting a difficult battle. Determined to be accepted and successful on the basis of her music alone, she has, to a degree, cut herself off from the mass audience, the ones who want to see a show. What Toni Brown shows is in the words she writes and the songs she sings.

I'd been working at a straight job at the University of California. I was writing songs all along—I'd been writing for some time—and I did some semiprofessional stuff. I played with a band in Berkeley. I got a bunch of songs together and played with a lot of different people, and was working to support myself. I don't know how, but I just decided, at some point along the way, that either I was going to do music or I wasn't going to do music. I was tired of what I was doing and I felt like I had something to say. I wanted to see how far I could go with it.

It was just about that time that I met Terry, and she had the same feelings I did. Her background was a lot like mine, we were both working at the same kind of job, we both loved music. We both knew who the other was, but we had never played together. After rapping with her, and knowing the situations we were both in, we decided to get a band together.

We knew nothing about rock and roll, we knew nothing about electric music. We were both folkies. In folk music, you don't notice that there is any chauvinism around, you're not aware of it. I was never aware of it. I grew up feeling like I could do pretty much what I wanted. It was sort of a natural transition to play electric music because that's what was happening then.

So we started out doing it, and what we played was sort of a hybrid of folk, folk rock, whatever we liked. We began to get a following, started playing in public, people liked it. There was still no problem as far as we could see. Being women seemed to be secondary to the music.

How did your career
in popular music get started?

Toni Brown / 33

Finally, the press picked up on the fact that there were two women on stage who were playing instruments and singing songs and sort of doing the whole thing, and wasn't that extraordinary? Then Terry and I stopped and took a look at it.

I remember in the early days of the band thinking that audiences were really going to dig what we were doing because it was new. I knew it was new, but I didn't realize how odd it was. It was the press that brought it to our attention. People who interviewed us would ask us what it was like. Women's liberation was pretty strong in the early days of our band, it was gaining momentum then, and I pooh-poohed it. I thought burning bras was a lot of horseshit. I can't identify with those people. I like men, I like being with men, I want a family and I want to be a wife and mother. There was always that feeling that I could do it all.

It was weird all of a sudden to be put in some kind of bracket and have to respond to questions like, "How do you feel about women's lib? Do you run into any male chauvinism? How do men react to you?" We started becoming aware of little things that happened. At first I guess I was apt to disregard it, I was more apt to say, "Oh, that isn't really happening, there isn't any male chauvinism in the business. The people at Capitol Records are treating me the way they would treat anybody else. And our manager may have trouble because Terry and I are both aggressive people, but he probably has trouble with aggressive men as well." I'd sort of just ignore it. It's only recently that I've become confused. I'm starting to wonder about it, because it hasn't really touched me directly.

I feel a lot of this stuff in the business goes on behind your back. My boss now at MCA, the guy I talk to, who is a friend of mine now, will say, "I'm just a chauvinist pig," and we'll laugh about it. But I know that he is behind me 100 percent, they're putting a lot of money into my album. I feel like I'm getting a fair shake, certainly more so than I did at Capitol. I feel like I could get a band together, if I really wanted to do that I have the authority to do it.

In Nashville, when I was working with the studio musicians there, they were wary at first, they didn't know me and I didn't know them, but there was a hell of a lot of respect. They were knocked out, I would say, by me and my music, and I became one of the boys to them.

In becoming one of the boys, do you think you had to sacrifice any of your feminity? Did you have to change your behavior?

No, but I'm not the kind of woman who has ever been conscious of that. If anything, I've had trouble being passive, I've had trouble letting men dominate me. I don't like being dominated. I don't like playing the flirty-cutesy role, and I'm not a doll-like figure. And I'm not a sexpot. There is a certain amount of it, but I've never played it up like some women have. I could never do that, it would be phony to me.

There were several occasions when it was pointed out to us. David Rubinson, the manager of the Pointer Sisters, told Terry and me, when he was thinking of producing us, that we'd better wear low-cut gowns, and why don't we get out there and try to turn people on, which turned us totally off and made us angry at him. Consequently, that and other things made it impossible to work with him. At the time I thought, well that's the way he is, some men are like that; they want you to get up there and shake your tits and ass. I'm not going to do it.

There have been other hints at that. People have told us we could really make a lot more out of being women on stage than we do. Well that's true, but there are a lot of guys who get out there and as far as I'm concerned most of the stuff they do is just macho bullshit. I'm not concerned with that, I'm concerned with making music, and relating to people, and communicating with them. If I'm communicating anything, it's that I'm not going to be put in some kind of category. If some men have trouble accepting that, well, I have trouble accepting some men. It works both ways.

I don't think I experienced any setbacks, any direct confrontations that hurt me, that put me down, because I don't let things like that hurt me. I'm beginning to get the feeling that the bad attitudes are behind the scenes in the record business, in the executive and merchandising branches, and dee jays. I'm very interested right now in talking to dee jays, because I think it is really a totally unconscious thing on their part that they do not play women's records. And there are not very many women signed to contracts. It seems as though they get in a pile of records and they look for the tracks that are the long, drawn-out instrumentals so they can go out and get a cup of coffee. Women don't play those things. Women don't jam on records, at least not yet.

Has that attitude hindered you at all?

I think they overlap. I think there are a lot of men who are making the same kind of music women make, but mainly men go to more extremes and that comes from instrumental expertise. There just aren't that many women yet who can play well enough.

*Do you think
there is an identifiable sound
that can be attributed to
women's music?*

I think it's a conditioned thing, and I think it is very subtle and unconscious. When rock and roll started out, it was strictly a vehicle for men. It was difficult for women to make the transition, plugging in and playing loud. I don't think it's a conscious thing at all. I think it's a question of, what are you used to doing? What are your usual alternatives? Singing is something else, I'm talking about playing.

Being a piano player and thinking about having some people back

*Do you think
women have been hesitant to compete
in that type of music?*

Toni Brown / 35

you up is not too great a transition. But playing guitar or bass or drums or sax is. I don't know quite why that is. There may be competition involved, feeling that there are so many men who are good at a certain instrument; but why isn't it there with singing, or anything else?

Did you ever study piano formally?

Oh sure, I studied classical piano for nine years. I'd also been interested in folk music. I really played both. I used the techniques I learned in classical to put together my own music. Much of what I learned to play came from listening to records and picking up on what I heard, going through the history of pop music really, from ragtime to jazz—so many things. I also liked country music a lot and listened to it a good deal, and jazz singers and gospel. There are a lot of different areas there. They were all influences.

Do you think there are certain consistent themes in your writing? Certain ideas you seem to come back to?

Yes, I do. I think there is the feeling of being abandoned, being left. As I externalize my music more and more, I can write about other situations. There is a strain of sadness, the theme of being an orphan in the world. I'm getting bored with it. I don't feel that way any more, although part of me maybe still feels that way. I've got a much more positive outlook on life.

Maybe it's in the social life area that I feel more of that male chauvinist attitude, sort of separating that from music. It was in the social realm that I suffered a lot of pain as a result of feeling that some men didn't take me seriously. Why can't I meet some guy who'll let me be me? Someone who'll accept me and not try to make me into something I'm not? Whether it's a sex object or whatever. I want to be me, and every time I try to do it, I'm threatened. Am I really too opinionated? Am I too aggressive? Can I be aggressive and be a woman? Those were things that were bothering me and that have bothered me over the years. But music was apart from that.

Do you think being a woman affects your point of view as a writer?

Yes, definitely. I've become a lot more aware of it. And I think there's a lot to be said about women's experiences. It's difficult for women to be taken seriously on a lot of levels. I think part of that is education. For a long time women didn't go to college, or if they did, they went to find a husband. That's changed.

I went to Bennington College, I was very lucky. Women were really taken seriously there. You leave Bennington and you feel, well I'm just like anybody else. I can go out and do whatever I want. It's disillusioning when you have a degree in literature and all you can find is secretarial work, and you can't type. Then that starts to work at you. You start to feel, well why did I do that? What is all this about? Four years of studying literature and writing poetry and there I am behind a typewriter? It's ridiculous.

I don't know, but I think he probably wouldn't stop at a bachelor's degree. If he really wanted to get into it, he probably could have gotten a job more easily at a publishing company doing editorial work, just sort of making his way gradually into the world of literature. I think a woman is more apt to be stuck in some little dumpy side office talking to executives and being pushed around. You've really got to have a lot of guts, you have to say to yourself, this is what I want and if they don't let me do it, I'll have to leave. You have to be able to somehow stand up to it, which I think is hard.

It goes even farther back than that. I think one characteristic of my generation of women is that a lot of the mothers are very confused women. They tend to think of themselves as children. They say, why do you have to struggle so hard? Always let the man win. Then they do things like drink themselves into some kind of state of mind where they feel good. When I see that, I get very angry. And behind all that, their husbands may be responsible. Why don't they help, why don't they include their women in their lives? Many of those women have nothing to do. Those are the kinds of things I think need to be said. That's what I try to write about in my songs. Some situations come from friends' families, some from my family, things that I see around me.

I think my experience is somewhat limited because I did come from an upper-middle-class background and I know that it's not like that all over. It's really bad at other levels where you can't escape the drudgery. I was lucky. I went to college, I had brains. I could stand up to it, and I let it roll off my back for quite a while, but I was unhappy for a hell of a long time.

What would a man with the same degree have done?

Yes, but I try to stay away from it, I don't like it. I don't like the "star" image, I don't like the groveling for the top that some people seem to do. I don't like the competition and the one-upmanship that seems to go on all the time. I saw a lot of that in the folk thing. You had a party with ten guitar players and everyone was trying to get attention. I just don't like it.

You read Random Notes in *Rolling Stone* and you get the feeling that there is a big incestuous mob that travels between LA and New York being seen in various places. That's bullshit. But for a lot of

Do you think there is a social scene that goes along with the music business?

people, they have to do it, they have to keep in the swing. They have to feel like they're part of it. They get a lot of gratification from it, but I don't feel that I'm that insecure.

Is it difficult to be married and yet pursue a career in music?

It hasn't been. I've been lucky. My husband is very open to it. But I didn't get married until I was thirty-three. We were both concerned, we thought about how it would affect our lives. But he's a filmmaker and he goes out on films on location, and I have to be by myself or I have to go out on the road, and we both know there has to be that freedom.

There isn't any reason, really, to get lonely. You can sit down and write a song about it, or go out and visit people. There are a lot of women who can't do that. They're just totally dependent on men. I just never felt that, I could never accept that.

How do children fit into that picture?

Well, we want children very much.

Do you see that as being any kind of hardship on you?

No, because I'm not that ambitious as far as getting out into the music world. I will always write music, I will always write songs. My main aim is to get my name out there enough so that other performers will know my work and record my songs and I can stay home.

So your main goal is to be known predominantly as a writer. How do you feel about performing?

I feel a certain pressure at this point because my album is going fairly well, and I know it's going to be necessary to do it. I enjoy that aspect of the business least. That's why I left the Joy the Cooking, because it got to be too much of a strain. But then people have told me that the conditions have never been right for me. With the right place, the right sound, if conditions were good, I might really dig it. There have been times when I really enjoyed it, and I think I probably always will do it to a certain limited extent. But I'm not going to jeopardize my family, I'm not going to leave a kid in a back room. That comes first to me and I think it always will.

How do you feel about your new album? How did it come about?

Well it came about like a fluke. I'd left Joy of Cooking, but I was still writing songs. Terry and I did the *Cross-Country* album in Nashville, but I wasn't really with the group any more. Then I got an offer from MCA and my first reaction was, People know who I am? Artie Mogull, specifically, whom I'd met at Capitol, wanted to sign me, and he ended up at MCA. I sort of let that happen. I didn't know if I could do it, make an album by myself. At first I thought I couldn't possibly do it, but it happened. There I was with the contract and I had to do an album.

I started out thinking I was really a writer, not a singer. Then I talked to a producer at Elektra who asked me why I was making a record, was I a singer or not? He said, "If you're not going to be a singer on this thing, no one is going to listen to you." And that really took me back. He said, "Well, if you don't feel like you're a singer, take some lessons."

I'd never thought of that, it never occurred to me to take lessons, or that I was a singer. So I thought about it and decided he was right. I thought, I'm going to have to take some lessons. So I did, and that really started helping me. It opened up a whole world of sounds I could make that I never was able to make before. It really helps. Now I think, God, why didn't I do this ten years ago?

Is it difficult for you to make your feelings known in the studio?

No, I had a great rapport with Chip Young, who produced my album. That had to be there. I couldn't work with anybody I didn't have that rapport with. I made a tape for him on a four-track machine that I have and I overdubbed all the harmony parts, and he was really knocked out by it. He used a lot of my ideas. If I had an idea I spoke up, but many times the guys who played on the album, and Chip, were so good that they opened my eyes to new things. I let them do a lot of their own things because I loved what they were doing. Anything I felt strongly about I said, and they would go along with it. In fact, they would ask me about things. Do you like that introduction? Is that the right beat? It was really a beautiful, relaxed working situation, which made the album really possible for me. If there had been any kind of tension, I think that probably I would have choked up.

How do reviews and criticism affect you?

Of course I'm flattered when anyone hears what I'm doing and says things that I really feel are right on. I like it. I get a little discouraged when they don't, but I don't let it bother me, I don't dwell on it. I just think that's one opinion and maybe that person isn't really hearing me. I get enough feedback from people who do like it, that it counteracts that.

With Joy of Cooking, I'd say 90 percent of the reviews were really favorable. I haven't really had the experience with somebody I respect saying that my work is bad. Some writers really write scathing, horrible reviews and a lot of what they say is really uncalled for. Fortunately, that's never happened to me. So much of it is subjective.

It's just nice to know you're reaching somebody, like I go downtown and the mechanic who works on my car says, "You make great music, lady. I've been hearing your record on the radio." That's what does it to me. That's so great.

How do fans react to you?
How do women fans react?

We've had some very close women fans, people who have kept in touch with us from the very beginning and still write us. Some of them were very upset when I left Joy of Cooking. They've followed our careers very closely.

I think we have some strong men fans, too. When we were playing around the Bay Area, some of them would appear at every gig. After a while, you start noticing that. I remember one night we played in Sacramento. The audience seemed to be predominately under eighteen, and there were two little boys right in front of the stage who were just swooning at each other because of us. They'd look at Terry and sigh and then they would look at me and sigh. They were just like little girl groupies, but they were teenage boys. It was really funny.

Are there any male groupies?
Did you run into any on the road?

Yes, I would say there are, like these guys who'd come to our gigs all the time. They would keep their distance usually. Most of them aren't about to try to get too close. Well, a lot of them do, they'd invite us to parties and we'd just politely refuse. Then there is a good deal of present giving. Fans make presents for you. And you get mail, crazy letters.

I would say our fans were fairly evenly divided: half of them were female and half were male. We certainly did get a lot of women's libbers, some of whom really turned me off.

Do you think
you will record with Terry again?

We both certainly hope we can. We did the Toni-Terry album, and the idea has always been that we each make our own music and then get together. When she gets a contract, we'd like to do another album together and then go on tour together. We'd like to get a road band, do some of my stuff, some of her stuff. We'd also like to go to Europe. Joy of Cooking never got the chance to tour in Europe. Who knows?

Toni Brown / 41

RITA COOLIDGE

Rita Coolidge is a lady who is finally at home. She has found a personal as well as a musical identity, and is at ease with herself and her life. She is dark and lovely, full of quiet confidence and well-being. When she sings, her voice is strong without edges, comfortable and fluid. On stage she uses it like an instrument, pointing and coaxing, warming an audience into a relaxed, collective smile of recognition.

It has taken Rita some time to find this ease. She moved to Los Angeles from Memphis where she had been singing in clubs with her sister Priscilla and recording radio jingles. A contract with Memphis-based Pepper Records resulted in her first hit single, "Turn Around and Love You."

In Los Angeles, she met Delaney and Bonnie through their mutual friend Leon Russell, and she was asked to sing on their first album. During those sessions, producer David Anderle became very enthusiastic about recording Rita as a solo. Until she could break her contract with Pepper, however, she had to be content with background vocal duties on albums for the likes of Dave Mason, Eric Clapton, Steve Stills, Leon Russell, John Sebastian, Al Kooper, and Graham Nash.

She survived Joe Cocker's Mad Dogs and Englishmen tour, and received a good deal of critical acclaim for her solo number, "Superstar."

Finally able to record on her own, her first album for A&M Records, *Rita Coolidge*, was released in early 1971. The influence of Cocker, Russell, and Delaney and Bonnie, led her to an undefined style and audience. She fell prey to pressures trying to fulfill other people's expectations. Rita recalls her first album with fondness. "It's a good album," she says now. "But someone else's good album." Even with its lack of cohesion, *Rita Coolidge* contains an exceptional version of Van Morrison's "Crazy Love."

As she became more independent, her music became more personal, resulting in a fine second effort, *Nice Feelin'*. The sound was more gentle, the energy level lower, the mood heightened. Her voice was emphasized and complemented by several fine musicians, notably drummer Sammy Creason and keyboard virtuoso Mike Utley, members of the Dixie Flyers with whom Rita toured. The album and subsequent road trip set Rita in the right direction, encouraged by her friend and extremely talented producer David Anderle.

Warmth and point of view are her gifts, shared with the feelings of identification. Material means little beyond its interpretation, the approach to a song becoming its life. Rita now sings only what she believes. Her third album, *The Lady's Not For Sale* amplified this image.

Early in 1972, Rita was preparing to leave for Memphis to rehearse with her band, when she met singer-songwriter-actor Kris Kristofferson at the airline ticket counter. They found themselves sitting next to each other on the plane. Kristofferson, on his way to Nashville to record, changed his plans in mid-air and went to Memphis with Rita. They started juggling their tour schedules so they could be together, and then they started appearing together on stage. Finally, Rita broke up her band and Creason and Utley joined Kris's group. Their musical and personal relationships complemented each other with great success.

Kristofferson, a former Rhodes scholar and gifted songwriter who has four albums on Monument Records, also has a burgeoning acting career. He has appeared in *Cisco Pike, Blume in Love,* and *Pat Garrett and Billy the Kid,* in which Rita played the role of Maria, her first acting assignment.

Rita and Kris were married in mid-1973 and shortly thereafter recorded their first complete album together, *Full Moon.* To Rita's surprise, it became a number one country and western LP. Ironically, she was born and raised in Nashville, but never considered herself a part of its country and western musical scene.

"I think 90 percent of the people in Nashville have never been to the Grand Ole Opry," she remembers. "They don't know where Music Row is. When I was little, I used to think that all those country and western people were just in town for the weekend."

When Rita was growing up, she sang in church choirs where her father was preaching, and in school choirs, often harmonizing with Priscilla. She has come a long way from her early years of scuffling.

Rita Coolidge tries to maintain an even pace, a perceptible balance between the hectic outside world, and her own personal choices. She seems unchanged by her growing popularity. She is openly enhusiastic, enjoying herself, but cautious in her optimism. she points toward Spring and new beginnings. Early 1974 brings a new house in Malibu overlooking the Pacific Ocean, the arrival of her fourth solo album, and her first baby.

I wanted to be an art teacher when I went to school. I got my degree in art from Florida State, and I really wanted to teach in elementary school. After I graduated, I looked around for a job in Memphis, but there wasn't much. It seemed like music and art teachers were the last ones to be hired. So I was living in Memphis and couldn't get a job teaching, so I used to paint school buses, and passed my talents around town painting people's cars and crazy stuff like that just to make enough money to live.

Then I found out about the Jingle Factory, Pepper and Tanner, so I went in there one day to audition. I'd been singing a lot in church and school choirs and I could sight read. I asked them for a job but they told me they didn't need anybody. I told them I wanted a tryout anyway so I could be on their waiting list. They let me audition that day, and I started working part-time.

We did mostly radio spots. They had packages that they sold to different areas, so we had to sing the same line, only with different call letters, all day long, over and over until we'd just about be stark raving mad. I was their last extra person, but every once in a while, I would get Priscilla in on it.

We were working nightclubs then, too. We were a sister act. She had a gold lamé dress and I had a silver lamé dress with red patent leather shoes. We used to sing at the Whirlaway Club in Memphis. We'd come out and do a floor show. Brenda Patterson was working there, too. We really went through some hard times at that place. A man died one night in that club while Priscilla was

How did you first become interested in popular music as a career?

singing. It's not funny, but I guess she really knocked him out. It was all a Mississippi and Arkansas crowd who'd come in for the weekend. It was huge place where people would gather after football games. I can't even remember the songs we sang. It must be a mental block. Mostly we did the regular Memphis stuff, like "Midnight Hour," and a couple of Bee Gees tunes. We did that for maybe a year. I was working both jobs and not having too much fun.

Then Pepper started their own record label, and I signed with them and made a single, "Turn Around and Love You." About that time I met Leon Russell, and he and I and Marc Benno came out to Los Angeles just to see what it was like. We came out for three days and never went back.

Then I met Delaney and Bonnie and that was that. I didn't even go back for my stuff. I had escaped and there was no way I was going to go back. Just about the time I left, I think Memphis really took a dive. At one time it was so huge. Chips Moman's studio was going all the time. People like Dionne Warwicke, Dusty Springfield, Joe Tex were all recording. There were about fifty Top 40 records in one year cut at that studio. It was really hot. Then I guess about that time, not too long after, people started going to Muscle Shoals and other places to record. There wasn't much left in Memphis but Stax Records and they were in trouble. I think Issac Hayes pulled them out of it.

It's hard to believe that five years ago, I was living in Memphis with Priscilla and Brenda and Priscilla's two kids and Brenda's kids, and another girl, Veniece Starks, who used to go on the road part-time with James Brown and sing at Elvis Presley's New Year's Eve parties. All of us were living in that house and starving to death. We could all sing, but that didn't necessarily mean we could get anywhere in Memphis.

We came out to LA in January of '68, and Delaney and Bonnie were getting ready to make their first album. We were over at their house one night when they were rehearsing, and just started to sing. They asked me to sing on their album, which was the greatest thing that had ever happened to me. A whole album, it was incredible. It's still my favorite Delaney and Bonnie album, one of my favorite albums in the world.

In the meantime, the record that I had cut back in Memphis had gotten to be a hit, which was really fun. I can't get a hit now for anything. It's so hard to get a record played. But they were playing that one on KHJ every hour. I guess I didn't realize how important it was. If I could only follow it up now, five years later.

Anyway, I was signed to Pepper and I couldn't record on my own. I had met David Anderle, who was supervising producer on the Delaney and Bonnie album, and I decided I wanted to work with him. But there wasn't much I could do. I went on the road with Delaney and Bonnie and did background sessions just to get by. It took almost two years to get out of my contract. By 1970 I was ready to do an album of my own when Joe Cocker called me to go on the Mad Dogs and Englishmen tour. I thought it would be good experience. Little did I know.

It was one of the hardest periods of my life. The tour was really tough. It's so hard for me to talk about it. It was pitiful. I was about fifteen or twenty pounds underweight when I came home. I weighed about 103 or 104, and I'm pretty good size to weigh 103 or 104. And I was a kind of a pale green color. We looked like we'd been locked in a dungeon for two months. I saw the movie when I got back and it was hard to sit through it, because I was still so close to it. You get fifty-five rock and roll crazed people together on the road, well, we started out at fifty-five, and ended up about thirty. It's no wonder with all the stuff that goes on with a community like that. Trying to travel, flying all night, sleeping in the daytime, two shows at night. It was miserable.

I really wanted to quit, and I did quit several times, and then I'd see Joe and he had the whole weight of everything on him because he definitely wasn't ignorant of what was going on. There was no way he could quit. I really felt close to him, and I felt that if I stayed, it might mean something to him. So I went through with it.

It was really tough. Some people came out with flying colors, but for most it was pretty hard. There were a lot of drugs and stuff going around, and the mass gonorrhea. I went down to the lobby one day and I guess half the crowd was lined up to get on the bus to go get shots. That kind of thing was going on all the time. People brought their kids along, and their dogs. The dogs were probably in better shape than anybody. But the kids had no business being there. The grownups had no business being there.

This many years later, I still get up on stage and somebody in the back screams, "Sing 'Superstar!' " I'll never sing that song again, even though I know it probably did help me, help people to know who I was. I haven't sung it since the tour and I won't sing it again. Everytime someone screams for that song I just get a cold chill. I want to tell them to shut up and listen to something else, like the thirty songs I've recorded since then.

The Cocker tour plus the whole Delaney and Bonnie thing had a big influence on my first album. Something I wasn't aware of then, but I'm aware of now, is that I was totally into Bonnie Bramlett's style of singing. It's amazing to go back and listen to it because at the time if people would have told me I sounded like her, I would have said they were crazy. But I did sound a lot like Bonnie.

On my first album, I was trying a lot of things, trying whatever I thought might work. First albums are so hard to do. I can't even remember recording it because recording is so easy now. When I went to make my first album, it was the biggest thing that had ever happened to me in my life, and I treated it that way. I was dead serious. I had to have all these people on it and it had to be huge. It had to be everything because at the time it was everything. Now I go into the studio with three or four musicians, piano, bass, drums, and guitar, and it doesn't even seem like work. David is so easy to work with, and so are Mike and Sammy from my band. We've been working together for so long, it's easy.

I feel lucky to have the relationship with my record company that I do. I know record companies don't necessarily treat artists the way A&M does, and they don't treat everyone the same. But I think part of the reason that they have been so good to me, is that I've been on the road for so long. When you're on the road, it's easier for them to sell records.

Do you think you had to work harder to get established because you are a woman?

I don't know. When I was establishing myself, none of this women's movement stuff was going on. I was never aware of it being harder for a woman until people started talking about women having a hard time. None of my recording problems came from a sexist thing. I have very few problems in the studio anyway, because the people I work with are my good friends. It's so close now it's like a family. I can't remember ever thinking "He's a guy, he doesn't understand." Music is so far removed from any of that. Music is a language, and if you're talking about the key of G, it doesn't matter if you're a man or a woman.

How do you feel about writing your own material?

I guess I'm just lazy. I get ideas for songs and I never seem to get past the first verse and chorus. I don't know why. Maybe it's easier for me to be lazy now because I'm married to Kris, and he's fabulous. I can sing the songs he's written.

It's really a lazy attitude to have and writing is something I want to do. I feel like I'm missing something by not writing. We go to Nashville, and people sit around and play their songs for each other, and I'd love to be able to do that, to play one of my songs for them. But I just haven't written any.

There's a lot of good material around, too, that hasn't been sung yet. There are also a lot of songwriters who don't necessarily sing that well, and I think some songs deserve very special treatment. To hear Maxine Weldon sing some of those songs is really incredible. She sings Bob Dylan's "It Ain't Me Babe," and it's like a brand new song. To be able to treat a song so specially is really nice. Until I start writing, that's what I'm trying to do.

People have called me to thank me for cutting their songs. It makes me feel so good when they do that. Frank Sinatra sent Kris a note thanking him for writing "Nobody Wins." It was such a nice touch for him to do that. I've made a point to play a song for a writer, but I've never written a thank you note. That's great.

Oh sure. Not by members of the immediate band, but by people who just come around. I think I'd like to keep it that way. I like my privacy, and I like to keep my business my business.

Is Rita the performer treated differently than Rita the person?

I'm losing my privacy now to a certain extent. Not to the point where I have to make myself unavailable. I know that I can still say no to a lot of things. Kris has always had a hard time saying no. He really had a hard time for so long trying to make it, and when guys come up to him now and ask him if he has time to listen to a song after a show, he just can't look at the guy and say no. Many times I end up going places with him that I would probably have said no to, especially when we're on the road and we go to someone's house, but I guess it means a lot to them.

Kris is going through a worse privacy thing than I am. It's one thing in music, but when you're in movies, it's just ridiculous. If he's got his beard, he's from *Blume in Love*, and if he doesn't, he's from *Pat Garrett and Billy the Kid*. He has no more disguises now.

More so to Kris, because I'm able to keep a certain distance. It's not hard for me to say "not now." We were in Odessa, Texas, once and there were about a hundred people outside the dressing-room door. Kris invited them all in. He felt that if they all came in we'd sign autographs and get it done more quickly. We were there for an hour and a half, with a dressing room full of fans. They want autographs and to ask questions. There's always fifteen people with tape recorders who you know don't write for anything and they just have that little scared look on their faces, and they ask, "What do you do for fun?" They don't bother me too much.

Are fans a problem?

Every once in a while, though, a person will come along who'll get it in his head that I'm the inspiration and guiding light and I have all the answers. That's pretty hard to deal with. I don't even know what all the questions are. I don't know any secrets. They want to know things like how did you make it, and what should I do now, and tell me how to make records. I really don't know what to say.

I mostly try to look like I'm not uncomfortable on stage, because for so long I was so uncomfortable that I tried to think of things to

Do you try to be sexy on stage?

Rita Coolidge / 51

do, like what to do with my hands. I was trying to work out steps, too, when I realized that all of it was getting in the way of the music. I had to drop all the dance routines and just try to sing the song.

Who do you think your audience is?
Whom are you singing for?

I sing for whoever has lived that song. People relate to songs according to their experience. But it's really hard for me to tell about my material now. We cut what we thought was a pop album, and it became the number one country album. *Full Moon* is not a country album to me. How do I know what I'm doing now? I don't know how it happened, but it's fabulous. I may be the queen of rhythm and blues tomorrow and have completely missed it.

Women buy records and women set trends. I'm sure I try to reach women. I always look at my girlfriends when I cut something to see how they are going to react to it. I really trust their reactions, maybe more than I would trust a man's reactions, because I'm singing it, and women are going to relate to it.

How do you feel about reviews?

Concert reviews used to be really important and now they just don't mean a thing. We can just about count on the fact that our best shows will get terrible reviews and our bad shows will get good reviews. Invariably, there seems to be somebody who takes up an entire article talking about Kris' leather pants and my legs and doesn't even mention the music.

Good writers are great. I really respect a writer who is able to shut out his own personal views of somebody and write a critical review. It's nice to have those writers talk about you, whether they like you or not.

Do you think
the press has created an image for you?

I imagine so. It's the long legged, smoky voiced Indian, I guess. I wore the clothes, and I sing the songs, so I can't really blame somebody for labeling it over and over. People still refer to me as the Delta Lady. I've even forgotten where it came from. I really have to stop and think about where it came from. It's one of those remotely related songs from way back. People do hang onto those things. It really doesn't have anything to do with me. It's just a title of a song.

Criticism doesn't seem to mean as much to me now as it used to. It used to mean a lot. It hurts when somebody says something really ugly, and they do still say really ugly things, but not very often, and it's easy to see where it comes from.

I used to do a lot of interviews. When I first started going out on the road with my band, I was always going to press functions and talking to people. We didn't sell any more records or concert tickets.

Rita Coolidge / 53

It was just a lot of knowledge that didn't mean anything that was getting around, so I just stopped doing interviews unless I really wanted to do them. It takes more out of you than you get back.

How do you see yourself?

The friends I had the first day I came to California are still my best friends. It's hard for me to realize sometimes, from the letters I get, what people think I am, what kind of life-style I'm accustomed to. I've got the same friends and my family doesn't treat me any differently.

I think of myself as a strong person. I imagine I'd have to be pretty strong to have made it through the last four years. It can get awful lonesome on the road. Charlie Rich has a song, "I Feel Like Going Home," about the feeling that you're just at the edge, and all you can think about is going home. All the traveling and being in a different town all the time, and doing shows at night, and trying to get some sleep, it all goes on for weeks and months at a time. There's never time to stop and think about where you've been and whom you've seen and what you've meant to those people. When you finally get home, you're exhausted.

Traveling with Kris has kept me from being lonesome, and he's the boss because I'd rather not be. It's hard for any person to make the decisions in the band. I imagine it's harder for a woman. But if the respect is there, they're going to listen to you. There is a certain kind of male ego thing. If I ever have to call down one of the guys in the band, even if I'm right, I think he's going to get defensive because it's a chick calling him down. There's no way to get around it. It would probably be the same if it was a guy in front of a band full of girls and he picked one person out. It's such a defensive thing.

I called down my guitar player one night because he had been drunk on stage. Really the whole band was. We had been sitting around for a long time waiting to play, and by the time we got on stage, everybody was wasted. When we were finally in the car, I was still yelling at him, and he took it for a few minutes and then yelled back, "I don't know what you're bitching about, you weren't hot shit tonight." He just laid into me, and everybody turned on him and said, "Don't you talk to her that way, she was the only one who was straight."

At the same time, it was like having a bunch of big brothers who constantly looked out for me. It was fabulous. I never had to worry about being by myself. I had five of my best friends with me and they really cared.

Do you have any specific career goals?

I would just like to be Peggy Lee, that's all. Really, I'd just like to be able to keep singing, keep making records. It's not important to make a huge splash at any time, as long as it can consistantly keep going. I guess you have to make a mediocre splash now and then to keep going.

What I do is my life and what I am. Being able to sing is a very special thing to have, and I really feel like a very lucky person to be able to do what I do. I love it. I don't think I would feel this way about anything else, about teaching school. I might be able to, but being able to sing is a special thing. That's the best part of my work, the actual singing. It's always a magic time. Even on the Cocker tour, as bad as it got, when the music was happening everything else was so unimportant. Joe was so fantastic and it was such a good band. The music would just clear everybody's heads.

The baby is definitely going to mean some more settling down, as far as being in the same place for more than a day. At the same time, I don't really do that any more anyway. At a certain point in my career it was important to be on the road, and hitting every town. It may be important again, but I think in the last year or two we've hit just about every town in the country, and I don't think we have to go back just yet. If I have somebody with me like a nurse who can take care of the baby, then I can do what I want to do. The baby is not going to hang me up. The baby is going to make me very, very happy.

How do you think
the baby will change your life?

Oh yes. I'm pretty happy right now. I really don't get depressed too much. I don't have that much to be depressed about. I really have a lot of things to be happy about. It's so good sometimes that I keep waiting for the bomb to drop. I have a great old man, a baby, I can sing, I have a fabulous family, a great record company, a good manager. Everything is OK. No part of my life is really a rotten egg. I'm just super lucky. I'd sure like to hang on to that luck for a while, too, because I've sure gotten comfortable with it.

Do you think
you are basically a happy person?

Rita Coolidge / 55

TERRY GARTHWAITE

Terry Garthwaite sits in the dim light of the Buena Vista Café in San Francisco, sipping an Irish Coffee and, in a characteristically serious way, continues to evaluate the problem of being a woman in rock and roll. It has been over two hours since the conversation began in a nearby hotel room. The change of scene has seemed to make her only slightly more at ease. Even the most casual observer notices the reserve—the intent, the educated, articulate dialogue.

Slender, with dark, undisciplined hair encircling her face, she smiles only rarely, but when she does, it lights her whole face, her expression softens and her body seems to relax. As quickly as the smile comes, it vanishes, and the reserve returns as if to protect her from revealing too much of herself. In a sense, the distance is a challenge, and in spite of it, Terry is amiable and friendly.

Born and raised in Berkeley, California, Terry spent two and a half years at the university there before she dropped out. Feeling as though she were going through her courses mechanically, she got a job at the Center for the Study of Higher Education where she says she was "a flunky for other people doing research." She kept track of test scores and IBM cards. Even though she found the work interesting, she spent evenings and weekends with her music, eventually playing and singing at folk clubs in the Berkeley area. She went back to school "piecemeal," and finally got her degree in sociology.

After spending a year in Europe, she returned home to find that the music scene had changed radically, and that rock and roll was pushing folk music off the stage. Curious about it, she was drawn to the electric guitar, putting aside her earier preference for acoustic music. In 1967 she met keyboard player Toni Brown through mutual friends, and the two of them became the nucleus of one of San Francisco's unique groups, the Joy of Cooking, unique in that it spotlighted two women, both of whom wrote, sang, and performed. They were also unusual in that their music was an interesting blend of folk, rock, country, and western, jazz, and Latin influences.

Joy of Cooking made three albums for Capitol Records, *Joy of Cooking, Closer to the Ground,* and *Castles.* Toni and Terry went to Nashville to do an album of their own, *Cross-Country,* which was well reviewed, but relatively unpromoted. After Toni Brown left the group, Terry reorganized the band and in late 1973 new musicians went into the studio to record a new album. That record, which Terry refers to so fondly, was the victim of the alleged vinyl shortage and some unresolved contract problems. As of Spring 1974, the album had no title and no catalogue number at Capitol and its release was unscheduled.

While her music has given her much satisfaction, Terry Garthwaite has had more than her share of frustrations at the hands of a male-oriented music business. At the time of this interview she was actively looking for a new record contract, determined to find an avenue through which to express her musical ideas. At thirty-five, she knows music will continue to be a part of her life, but she is reluctant to join the ranks of street musicians who are so visible at places like the Cannery at San Francisco's Fisherman's Wharf.

She sees herself as "a pretty good rhythm guitar player with tons to learn," and has an honest desire to sort out the place of women in rock and roll. In a letter I received from her shortly after our interview, she wrote:

It occurs to me that the importance of women in rock today has to do with women 1) playing instruments and being taken seriously as actual musicians, and 2) making meaningful statements about women's feelings through and around music, rather than the traditional statements which have frequently been put in the mouths of women by male writers. For women to be exploiting their own sexuality (which at the very least is a given) as a means of getting a so-called foot in the door is falling prey to the old set-up. If women are serious in their efforts as musicians, then let the world know it's their music and its message that merits attention, and it should speak for itself. Whatever advantages of being a woman will then be a bonus. Self-exploitation of the stereotypical women's wiles only confuses the point of women in rock. Women have been in music through history, but within rock they've been able to emerge as serious and articulate musicians/writers, speaking to and for a large audience.

Her concluding thought was provocative: "How much easier it would be with more women in all facets of the business, including record-store owners, publicity agencies, rack jobbers, deejays, engineers, producers and of course record company executives. Can you imagine?"

For Terry Garthwaite, imagining a music business like that augurs well. She is so deeply committed to her music that she seeks answers to some very complex problems while still maintaining a good degree of optimism. Perhaps the woman who seems so detached, so distant and reserved, finds herself much more personally involved in these issues, holds them closer to her, than people suspect.

Rock and roll was sort of a natural progression for me. I grew up in Berkeley. I've played guitar since I was about twelve. Not many people were playing guitar at the time in Berkeley, especially not folk guitar. There was a pretty heavy folk scene in Berkeley around the late '50s and early '60s.

*Would you begin
with some background information:
where you grew up
and how you got into rock and roll?*

One group was "purist," in a funny kind of way. They did bluegrass music, and they didn't do the kind of tunes that Joan Baez might do. In that sense, they might consider themselves purist. I was much more apt to be doing folk music that Joan Baez would do, Burl Ives tunes, or Josh White. My older brother sang and played guitar, and I was interested in whatever he was interested in. Also in those days, I used to listen to some jazz vocalists, Chris Connor and Mose Allison. We used to go to the Coffee Gallery in North Beach and listen to jazz in those days.

There were two clubs in Berkeley, the Cabale and the Jabberwalk. The Jabberwalk was where Country Joe and the Fish got started. During the time I was playing there, there wasn't any rock and roll happening. I left and went to Europe for a year, and during that time, Big Brother and the Holding Company got started, and Jefferson Airplane. It must have been 1965.

Toni Brown was also involved in this purist scene of doing bluegrass and singing country tunes. There were a lot of good musicians in Berkeley, mostly guitar and banjo players. I think because the university was there, a lot of people were drawn to the area, therefore a lot of interesting people were around. A lot of them were musicians and they drew people on the fringe. It's still that way. Obviously though, people come to Berkeley now for reasons other than the university, but I think it was responsible for a lot of the people who came there initially. The scene there used to be a lot smaller.

I guess for a long time I wanted to play music with other people. Even when I was just playing guitar and singing, sometimes my brother would come and play, sometimes I would play with another guy named Don Crawford. There were rock bands getting started. When I was gone in Europe I knew about this thing happening, and it was happening in England, and I was really curious about it. When I came back, sometime within that year, I met Toni through some other musician friends.

We started playing some tunes together. She had written a bunch of stuff and I had started writing when I was gone. It was fun. We jammed some and we jammed with my younger brother who was starting to play bass then. We thought, why not get some people together and see what happens. The three of us, plus Ron Wilson who was a conga player Toni knew, got together for about six months. We didn't know what we were doing. None of us had played rock and roll before, we'd all played whatever our kind of music was, so this was a way of bringing all these influences into one room. Then we tried playing with a trap drum and that really turned us on and we had to have one. Then we finally found Fritz Kasten.

There was one period before we got our trap drummer when we made a tape for the head of Arhoolie Records who was a friend of ours. It was partly for us, too, because we felt we had solidified something in our tunes. Then Toni went down to Los Angeles and took the tape to Mo Ostin at Warner Bros. Records. He wasn't too interested in it, but he was real interested in playing Tiny Tim for her. It was a failure, but I think it was very brave on Toni's part to take that tape in hand. So on the basis of that, we realized we weren't quite ready, and went back and worked some more.

We did play at some parties. Hideous parties. I hate playing for private parties. We played at one where everybody was supposed to come dressed as a hippie, and we were the hippie band.

What kind of tunes were you doing?

They were all ours, except for some traditional stuff, gospel music, some country-flavored stuff. Some of the tunes are on our first album.

All this started in late '67. By 1968, we felt we were ready enough to be a band, to go play somewhere. So we went to Mandrake's, which was our favorite club in Berkeley. There was no door charge, it was like we were auditioning for the club. All our friends came, the place was packed. We had a wonderful time.

Yes, I think we were. The first few times we played before we went to Mandrake's, as I said, we played at parties. We played at the gallery opening for a painter friend of ours, and that turned into a kind of happening. We all just put down our instruments and started clapping and dancing. Those kinds of things in the beginning gave us a warm feeling about what we were doing, and that feeling was shared with the audience. And that's what happened once we went to Mandrake's. We had that same kind of feeling. We played there for a couple of years, '68 and '69, or '69 and '70, probably a couple of times a month, one night at a time. We played occasionally at other clubs, too.

Probably after about a year of that, and playing in the park at San Francisco on occasion and some other local things and lots of benefits and farmworkers things, we decided to get a manager. Toni knew Ed Denson, who was manager of Country Joe and the Fish, so we approached him and told him we were ready to go find a record contract and we wanted a manager to do that. I don't know how we had that much sense. That was our choice in the beginning. He was the only guy around whom we knew who was a manager, and he was a lovely person, and he seemed to have done well for the Fish. So he started managing us.

I don't know how other people go about finding a manager. I suppose it's probably nice if some manager has seen you somewhere and approaches you because he is interested in your music. That kind of perspective would be meaningful because if somebody identifies with your music and really feels strongly about it, then he's going to work for it and he'll have an understanding of where you're coming from. I think Ed did to a certain extent, partly because our music was very people oriented and came out of the San Francisco Bay area. It was kind of laid back and Ed is that kind of a guy. So I think there was a certain amount of empathy. At the same time, I know he often went to sleep at our gigs, which was kind of a drag. But I couldn't expect him to listen to all of them.

Anyway, there were mistakes along the way, and sometimes it's hard to know what they were. How can you ever have the ideal situation? In fact, until you're really through the whole thing and looking in retrospect, you can't really know what the problems were.

While we were with Denson, we got a contract with Capitol Records, which he felt was a good contract. I think it was all right. Capitol turned out to be a very conservative company and not very hip to what's happening in the music scene, especially rock and roll.

We had a production company, and this I think was probably suggested by the manager, possibly because there were five of us who were equal partners in the band. The production company was us. What happens is that the record company allots a budget. They say, "OK, here is some money, go make a record and turn in the master," which is great because it does give us control over what we want to do on the record.

Were you calling yourselves The Joy of Cooking then?

Probably our first mistake was not having a lawyer look over our management contract. We trusted him and actually that was a mistake. He is not managing us anymore. We did work things out all right because he is a nice person. But it is always a mistake not having a lawyer if you're going to be signing your name to anything. I know a lot of people who have fallen into that worse than we did. There are so many money grubbers in the business.

None of us had ever made a record before, really, so we were all fresh to it. Denson, of course, had involved the Fish in making records, but I don't know who produced them. Our mistake here was not being aware of what a producer does, wanting really to do our own record, wanting it to be a representation of what our live music was, which meant trying not to do very much overdubbing, not having strings and horns, which means it was pretty funky. Well, that's all right. If you want to make a record that's going to be popular then I think there is a certain amount of production effort that has to go into it.

Did Capitol assign a producer to you?

That's what happened. We didn't know how to get a producer so they suggested one of their staff producers. He is about forty-eight years old, a lovely person, really nice guy, very laid back, very quiet. He's produced a lot of Frank Sinatra albums, old stuff like that, not too much recent stuff. I don't know why they assigned him, except that he was a very respected producer at Capitol. So he came up and talked to us, he listened to our music and he liked it. He made some suggestions, and we liked what he said. It was very comfortable working with him. He really didn't participate in arranging anything. Whatever ideas we had, we sort of went on with. We did our first album in San Francisco on a pretty down-home basis because there wasn't really much of a budget. I played clarinet on one tune doing some horn lines with Fritz, the drummer, playing saxophone. That was the extent of the horns on that album.

There were a lot of creative people working at Capitol, in the art department and the promotion department, who were excited about our album. It was a fresh sound and they liked it, so they worked their butts off and we thought they did some really nice stuff. That album sold well for a first album, and they picked a single that got on the charts.

How they picked that single, I don't know. That is something I've never known. I think that is another mistake we made, although I don't know what more we could have done. I know some record companies have meetings every week to decide which will be a single from which album. Capitol doesn't. The producer says, "Oh, this is a nice tune, I like this tune, this will be the single." That's just not a very hip way to go about it.

Record companies want to sell records, so you'd think they would try to pick something that would be appealing to the public out of the gamut of stuff we have on a record. God knows not all of it would be appealing to the masses, which can be a problem. It's been a problem for me because a lot of the music that I end up doing is kind of down home. It isn't very pop sounding.

Anyway, our first album came out in early 1971. By that time, we had been together three years. Along about that time, and this is another mistake we made, we had problems within the band musically and personally that we couldn't work out. Up to that time, we had been able to work out all of the problems we had come across, and there were a lot of problems. In some ways a group is a family, in some ways it's a marriage, in some ways it works like group therapy.

Not me. I think Toni and I were both leaders in different places. In rehearsal, Toni had a lot of definite ideas about how she wanted her tunes, instrumentally and rhythmically. I frequently had problems with that, not really knowing and being open to jamming and feeling my way through it. I think because I'm a lot more improvisational than she is, I'm better at just stepping out and doing it than somehow just having it all in my head.

I was the leader more on stage, partly because I was out in front. Toni was more behind the scenes in terms of arranging tunes.

Again, another mistake, and I think this is partly because we were women. We didn't want to say, "OK, you guys, this is our thing," although I think that is how it became apparent. In the very beginning it was a band kind of thing, although it was all Toni's and my material that we were doing. It was open to everybody to participate in, and it was a group feeling. We all enjoyed playing with each other. We always felt that it was an equal thing. The lines became clearer as time progressed. The guys did not participate in arranging tunes, they would sit back and wait. Occasionally there would be rehearsals where, just to see what would happen, Toni wouldn't say anything, or I wouldn't say anything. There would be no rehearsal.

That's one way it became clear who the motivators were. And yet the guys would resent it when the band began to be labeled a women's band, and there was the implication that it was not an equal group.

Do you feel like you are the leader of the group?

Did they ever confront you and say they didn't want to take orders from women?

No, never any confrontation like that, probably because it would be somehow too threatening, and I think they did enjoy the music, and I think they enjoyed playing with us, and I don't think they felt that threat strongly enough to jeopardize being in the band.

My brother played bass on the first album, and he felt that kind of thing. He felt his way of thinking about music wasn't being expressed. And we felt that his playing didn't fit in with what we needed. It became a musical conflict we couldn't work out, so we parted company after we recorded the first album, but before we went on the road.

Our manager knew about it, but somehow this information didn't get passed along to Capitol. When the people in the promotion department found out, they freaked. They were worried about who the band was going to be that went on the road. And we didn't realize the importance of having this unit to be able to follow up the album.

That is something I think management has to say. They have to say, "Look band, this is what's going on with the record company, your record is out, and you've got to follow it up by a tour if you want that record to sell." Nobody ever made that clear to us. We just didn't think about it. We didn't understand the logistics of putting out a record. Not that I do yet, mind you. It's so intricate. So we kind of blew it. We did eventually get somebody and we did go out on the road.

How do you feel about traveling, about playing on the road?

I like to travel, and to be in different cities. It's fun to play in different places. I don't like traveling when the tour is not set up comfortably, when we have to drive long distances. Our tours were never comfortable and that created a lot of tension.

Do you think being on the road is harder on women than it is on men?

I think probably that depends on the context that the woman is in. For me and Toni, it wasn't too bad. If I had been the only woman in the band, it would have been a lot harder than it was. I had a companion who I could hang out with, which meant that I didn't have to hang out with the guys and go to bars or whatever it is guys like to do. And I didn't have to sit alone in my hotel room.

All of the guys who have passed through our band have been really nice people, for the most part people who I've enjoyed being with. But still, when you're on the road and there's all that time when you're not playing, I like to have somebody I can go shopping or checking out antique shops with. Toni and I like to do a lot of that same stuff, and it made it fun.

66 / Terry Garthwaite

*Did you find that
promoters and club owners tried to
take professional advantage of you
because you were a woman
in front of a group?*

I didn't have much dealing with promoters. No, in fact, I found that a lot of times people have been very friendly. Most of the time we had a road manager who would meet all those people. I think a lot of times people backstage have wanted to make it very comfortable for us. A lot of times they haven't.

Rock and roll is set up for men. Your dressing room is the men's locker room, and you can't get away from the smell of a urinal. That's just representative. Why don't they use the women's locker room? Well, that's obvious. Or why don't they have a separate room where, if there are women in the band, they can go? There just isn't that kind of thinking. The obvious reason for it is that rock and roll is mostly men, although gradually, slowly, it's beginning to change a little bit. Also the promoters and other people connected with shows are usually men.

*Were audiences surprised to
find a group with two women in front?*

Yes, frequently there was surprise. I've heard comments like, "Oh my God, a chick playing guitar," or "Is that thing really plugged in?"

Guys have jumped up on stage and tried to participate. Partway through a set when they get to feeling the rhythm, they jump up and grab the maracas out of my hand. I think it's something they probably wouldn't do if it were a guy up there. It was kind of a takeover thing. I don't think it's malicious, but they wanted to be a part of things and the easiest thing is to say, "Move over, chick, I'm going to do this." That's kind of a message that I've gotten. It hasn't happened for a while, but it did happen several times.

Why did The Joy of Cooking break up?

I'm not even sure that it has broken up. For the last year, since Toni quit, we've been touring quite a bit around the country, and we owed Capitol an album, so we put one together. It took me a while to find a new producer. I found a guy who I was really happy with and he really felt my music. For our first three albums, we had this other producer, but with the new producer I feel we did better. I feel close to our newest record, I feel good about it. It was something that came out of me, it was really my music.

After Toni quit, I had to create a new band for the most part. It was a difficult thing to do, and it took some time. It was scary, because the Joy of Cooking had been based as far as I was concerned on the nucleus of me and Toni, the music that we wrote, mostly her tunes at one point, the harmonies that we did together, her keyboard playing, and my guitar playing and vocal trip on stage.

So I had to find a new keyboard player. I didn't want to replace Toni, I didn't want to try to recreate something. I wanted to have a band that could express my musical ideas. But it took a while to figure out what would feel good, it took a little juggling. Even now I have a better idea of what I would want. The Joy of Cooking changed from what it used to be, became something else, and my idea of what that could be is clear.

While recording the newest album, people from the record company would come by the studio and they seemed very excited about the music. Our old producer visited us. He was concerned all along, and he is a lovely guy. One night the guy who was the head of A&R came by and had a good time and said he liked what he heard. During the sessions, there was a good feeling.

The album was completed and coincidentally our option period was up. What happens at this point is that the finance committee steps in. The finance committee admittedly has little relationship to A&R, to the artists. Their decisions are not based on music or the artists, but strictly on finances. The Joy of Cooking's records have not sold that well since the first one. I don't think that's the fault of the music.

The Toni-Terry album, *Cross-Country*, which was a Nashville thing we asked please could we do, they simply didn't know what to do with it. The didn't know how to promote it so they didn't promote it. Somebody scribbled off an ad and sent it to *Rolling Stone.* I was really angry about how they handled that because there wasn't any interest in it.

Anyway, when we finished this last album, the finance committee said, "OK, look. If we're going to pick up your option we're going to have to give you a bunch of money in front, plus we just put money into the record, plus we're going to have to put money into promoting it if we put it out. We want to suspend your contract, put out the album, see how it does and if the folks like it, then we'll pick up your option." This was going to take about six months.

This is where I part company with a record company. If they are going to sign an artist, somebody ought to be interested in the music. If they're not interested in the music, then what's all the bullshit? I don't have a contract now because I'm off Capitol and I'm glad to be off because I feel that they really gave me the runaround. I'm looking for another contract. It's not easy to find.

I have a lawyer I rely heavily on for advice, because I don't know anything about this business, except what I've bumped up against. I've made a lot of mistakes, which is not to say that he doesn't make mistakes, but I don't feel like I can do it all myself. I need somebody for another perspective.

Fritz and I were doing most of the work this past year. We didn't have a road manager and he would go pick up the money and be sure the gig was set up right. There was a period where we were

Are you making your own managerial decisions now?

looking for another manager and we would go together to talk to people. But at this point, it's up to me to decide what I want to do. I do get advice from my lawyer. He's looking for a contract for me. I know it isn't easy.

How do you feel about the whole music business and the whole music scene?

I don't like the business of it, and I don't like the scene of it very much at all. The two things I like best about the music business don't have anything to do with the business except that I'm involved. One is playing for people and the kind of exchange that happens. This is more true in my hometown and has been more true in the past than it has away from home in a big place where nobody knows you.

That reminds me of the tour we did after our first album. Who'd ever heard of the Joy of Cooking? We would open bills a lot. OK, here are these two chicks up there singing their own tunes. You got a conga drum, why don't you play like Santana? You got a chick who can boogie, why doesn't she sing Joplin tunes? This was a typical kind of response we got.

This last year when we went out, we went to some places again where people had never heard of us, where they, in fact, did not see much rock and roll and were hungry for it. But they didn't know how to respond to this music, which was not familiar. I'm not saying we're totally new, but if I start scatting, again that's unfamiliar territory.

I remember one gig that we played, I think it was somewhere in the Midwest, and the people were just sitting there. At one point I jumped down off the stage. It wasn't very high. I wasn't either. I think it was in a gym, and there were a lot of people there, and I wanted to get closer to them. So I got down off the stage with the microphone and still nothing. That's really frustrating. When we were an opening act, there was a lot of that kind of thing. It was frustrating, but I think it also brought us together as a band. At that point, you realize that you have to believe in your own music, and you shouldn't feel as though you have to meet other people's expectations because they don't know who you are. By that I mean they don't know what you're feeling or what you're saying.

Some people I think have to have some kind of introduction, which probably begins with the promotion department of a record company saying, "OK, this is the Joy of Cooking and this is what they do."

Somehow if that gap of unfamiliarity is bridged, then there is a basis for communication. That was one of the hardest problems I faced in the early days.

The most important thing to me is the feeling that comes through doing the music, and as much as that can be exchange with the audience, the more I like it. That's what it always was when we played at Mandrake's. Hometown people came there and they knew our music and they liked it and they danced, and it really felt good. And that gets me off, that's what I feel is an exchange of energy, and to me that's the high point of music.

The other thing that I really like doing is making records, which is totally removed from people. It's very creative in a different way from being spontaneously creative with an audience, because you can overdub and you can experiment with different things. It's exciting being in the control room and putting a record together. I don't think I could ever do it myself, I don't think I could be a producer. One thing that interests me is the fact that there are very few women in production.

No, I don't think anybody has really laid that kind of a trip on me. I think early on there were some people who made some passing comments to that effect. I like to look nice on stage, but it's got to be my own style and not somebody else's image of what's glamorous. I like to wear flowing things, and I'm just starting to get into rhinestones and sequins and things like that. On stage is where you can wear a lot of that stuff.

*Has there been any
pressure on you to be glamorous
since you are up front in the band?
Has anyone wanted
to create an image for you?*

Because I make my own choices, I would say no. If it were interfering, then I wouldn't do it.

*Has being in the music business
affected your personal life, your
ability to have constant relationships?*

That's a hard question to answer. I don't think I feel competitive, but I find myself occasionally falling into certain situations. If I'm jamming with some guys and it occurs to me that I'm the only woman there playing an instrument, sometimes I think, OK, these guys are going to want to have their way with the music. If I have an idea about doing the music, or if maybe I feel somebody should play a solo in some part, I'll sometimes check myself and not say anything because I'm not going to tell these guys what to do. A lot of times I don't feel that way because I've always played with both men and women. In Berkeley there were always a lot of women musicians. In the folk scene, there were women around playing guitars, too, and also there was another woman in my band. So for me, it's something that I don't think about very often.

I once sat in with some people on a tune in a local coffee house, where there was a woman playing and singing, I was playing and singing, there were some guys playing, there was a horn player, a lead guitar, and I guess Toni was playing piano. I found myself, as

*Do you feel competitive
with men in the music business?*

soon as I finished singing the verses, saying, "OK, you solo," because I knew, and I think it comes from rehearsal, that if I didn't do it, nobody was going to do it, and everybody was just going to be up there jamming away. It's too messy, I don't like it that way. It just disintegrates for me when that happens. So I found myself telling people what to do and then I found myself thinking, who am I to be telling them what to do? Then I realized that's what I've had to do in our rehearsals.

Do you feel any pressure on you to be one of the guys? To communicate with male musicians on their own terms?

I don't think of it that way. It's hard to say. Am I being one of the guys, or are we all being musicians together? That's what it gets down to, when you are playing music and there aren't those kind of delineations drawn. When I am playing with the Joy of Cooking, I am one with all these people because we all are playing this music, but I also have to be in charge to some extent. I don't know how much they would agree with that statement, and in a way that's kind of an overstatement. I'm in charge in that if there is any confusion on stage, I will try to alleviate that confusion by making it clear what's going on. Because I am up front, I can do that, and also because it's my music.

Do you think you have been an example for other women?

Yes, I think both Toni and I have been. I know it's been true for some people; they have told us. When Toni and I started, like I said, it evolved for both of us. It wasn't that we deliberately wanted to put together some kind of a band that was focused around women, but it was, it evolved that way and people picked up on that. It seems natural to me that other women would be encouraged by seeing somebody who does play and is not afraid to be up front, out in front of men playing, and in fact not even having men soloing in the band, which again was not something that we were really conscious of when it was forming. However that's how it came out and it was all right.

I think there is a lot more empathy from women, and a lot more readiness to accept, very much so.

Has the woman's movement made you think about it more, more than you did when the band first got together?

Oh yes. I don't know that it's changed my thinking as much as it has clarified some of it. I do become aware of myself thinking in stereotypical terms, or I find myself shrinking back because I should be in the woman's place.

I'm not saying that changes my behavior in a situation, it's just that I become aware of it. Maybe it does change my behavior.

Maybe I'll still be aggressive, although I'll find myself thinking I should not be. If you want to call that being aggressive. I mean, is certain behavior aggressive if a guy does it, or is it only aggressive if a woman is trying to get things together?

Do you think things have been harder for you professionally because you are a woman?

I wish I knew the answer to that. I really don't know. Sometimes I wonder how anyone gets anywhere in this business, especially if you're a little bit odd. I don't mean personally, because if you're a little bit odd personally, you've got it made in this business. I mean if musically, somehow, you're not in the mainstream, and that's also true of women, because women in this business are not in the mainstream. That has become complicated in some ways because I think some people are more interested in women in bands just because they are odd and because they are faddish. It hasn't become so faddish though that people are on your doorstep wanting to sign you up. I'm sure some people in record companies still pooh-pooh women playing music, a lot of guys pooh-pooh women playing music, and guys have, behind my back pooh-poohed me playing music. From comments that my drummer has let slip, there are guys who did not want to come audition for us, who were not interested in jamming with us because there were women in the band.

It's too bad that there are some people who are so distorted in their socialization process as they're growing up that they somehow can't open themselves to experiencing women in some other way than what their stereotype of women is. Or conversely, that they can't experience musicians as musicians. I will never forget a comment made by a guy who worked in a music store. I had gone in to buy strings for my guitar or something, and somehow we got to rapping a little bit. I said that I was in the Joy of Cooking and he said he had seen us once at Mandrake's, and when he closed his eyes, he realized that we really were pretty good after all, as long as he could forget the fact that there were women in the group.

Do you have any specific goals now as far as your career is concerned?

No. At this point my goal is to get a record contract so I can feel that I have somewhere to express myself musically. I'm a singer more than I am a guitar player, but I don't want to stop playing guitar. I really like it and it's a part of my music. I like to put the guitar down and just get into a singing trip sometimes, and I focus more on singing. For me my goal is to be a better singer and to be able to get my singing out, to get it on a record, and to tour, to play for people.

I don't think I have any personal material goals. There is no end point that I can see in that respect. For me, most of my goals are centered around the music that I do. I'd like to be able to have recording stuff in my home, so that I wouldn't have to go out of my home to record. I like to be at home. I don't mean just by myself, I like to be there and I like to be centered there. I'm a Cancer, for whatever that's worth. It seems to hold true for me. But you have to go out and play. Like I said, I don't mind doing that, so it works out well.

Are most of your friends in the music business?

No, not in the music business, but most of my friends play music or sing. I don't have very many friends in the music business. As for a lot of people in the music business, except for musicians, I don't trust them. There's too much hype, and too much hustle for me.

Do you lead a fairly regular scheduled life?

There's no schedule at all. It pisses me off when you read about the government taking certain measures to conserve energy and how everything falls down according to the 8 to 5, Monday through Friday schedule. Anybody who's involved in the entertainment business in any form, or the recreation business, gets hit by those kinds of things, because we live backwards lives to those people. That is, I guess, how most people live, but thank God, I don't.

Is your career really important to you? Is there anything else you might consider doing?

Music is really important to me. I will probably always be a singer, and if I can earn my keep by playing music, that's how I want to do it. I enjoy doing that more than anything else. There are other ways I could scuffle by and would if I had to. But the best way for me to do that is through records, to have that kind of a way to approach it, to be able to work up tunes, make a record and sell those records, rather than singing at the Cannery out on the street. I'm not likely to go do that. I might, but not likely. I like to play in local clubs occasionally around the Bay area, and I do that once or twice a month, and that's for fun. I could go back to just playing music on my own. I'll always play music.

Do you feel you want to be thought of as a musician first and foremost?

It's hard to rank order those things. Am I a woman first or a musician first? I'm probably a woman first. I think my music says that too. And in that sense it's important not to always be a musician when you are with musicians, and in that sense, I'm really not.
I think that when women are playing music with men, there's probably something that happens in the music that you're not really aware of. I also think that's true in the music business. A lot of times

it's hard to know whether problems arise because you're a woman or for other reasons which you'll never know. There are some things which are more obvious than others. I think also, when you're a woman who doesn't fit the stereotype of somebody who's in the music business, and there are a lot of pigs in the music business, that creates problems.

Well, women should be what I call "chicky-poo," they should be ultrafeminine and be submissive in their attitude. That's not necessarily always true. I suppose I've felt that if I'm being who I am and asserting some idea which a man in the music business doesn't agree with, that he would be offended, somehow his hackles would rise, rather than being able to really discuss it as a valid idea. That's one example of a situation I might find myself in. Also men want women in the music business to be attractive in a certain way. That's not simple to do, but it's a simple concept, a simple-minded concept. The music business is just a funny, funny space to live in.

What do you think that stereotype is?

In that context, I don't think that I appeal to most guys in the music business because I don't think that I fit their stereotype. Maybe part of that has to do with the fact that I'm not interested in them in any way except businesswise. I'm not really sure what kind of women they're interested in. I suppose part of my concept of that has to do with comments that they make, maybe, in my presence. But then I am around them because I am an artist and I have business dealings with them. I'm not around them because they're taking me to lunch, although they may be taking me to lunch.

If that is the stereotype, where do you think you fit in? What kind of image do you have of yourself?

Yes, I think so to some extent. I think it's a vestige of what we all grew up with. I don't think I can totally get away from it. Sometimes it bothers me. Hopefully that won't always be true. I think probably over the years it's less and less true.

Do you find yourself competing with that stereotype?

Yes, I think that's probably true, that things don't seem to rattle me as much as they used to. I don't get uptight about some things which used to bother me. Again, I guess that's because sooner or later you realize that your own perspective is all right. It may not always be all right, it may not always work.

There is another facet of this whole business that perplexes me.

Do you find that as you grow older, things don't rattle you as much as they used to?

First of all, the music business is pretty broad, rock and roll is pretty broad. It's hard to say where music is going from here because I think it's kind of scattered. A lot of it is going into glitter rock or whatever you want to call it, and a lot of it is becoming very theatrical which is very far removed from where I'm at, although I would dig to wear groovy clothes on stage. My music is the thing that I'm saying, and it comes from the heart, and I can't clothe it in theatrics. I can clothe myself in something that makes it as visually interesting as it is musically, maybe, but that whole theatrical bit doesn't make sense to me. I can appreciate some of it, maybe, for the theatrics, but it doesn't have anything to do with music for me or for the kind of music that I like.

I feel partly that way about a lot of hard rock too, that a lot of the point of hard rock is its visceral effect on people. To me, music is too emotional to be taken lightly, if you can say hard rock is light. And it scares me when I see that kind of music, although I guess partly what scares me about it is the audience that is being fed it.

I think this stuff is popular for various reasons. One reason is the amount of hype which is behind it, the other reason is kids who are on drugs need to be bombarded by sound, or bombarded by something which is more than what's just musical or they're not going to feel it, and that's really scary.

At one of the early gigs we played in the Modesto-Fresno area, the kids were so stoned on some kind of downer, I don't know what they were on in those days, that they could not lift themselves off the floor. I don't enjoy that kind of atmosphere. I don't like to be part of that atmosphere. I don't like to see kids doing that to themselves. That's partly why for me the music that we have played has always felt best to me at a place like Mandrake's where there is also energy in the audience. It doesn't have to be real hyper energy. It's just an up feeling.

How do you feel about drugs?
Do you take drugs?

No. I smoke grass sometimes, but not very often. That's all. I don't like drugs. I especially don't like them when I play. I don't even smoke grass when I play, because I forget what I'm doing and I flash on things. A few times I've gotten stoned before I've played. I did once in Aspen, Colorado, and I felt like I was in Las Vegas.

I like playing in an atmosphere where I feel like I'm not the only one who's working or playing or there. I like people to participate from the audience. In some ways those down audiences drain energy from you, because God knows they need that energy, those people who are lying down there on the floor.

I think that the whole drug culture thing is a crying shame. I understand a lot of it. I understand it coming from parents who have been eating drugs for so long. Kids see their parents do it and feel why shouldn't they do it too? The parents don't have any conception of there being any similarity.

No I don't think that it's going to go away very soon. I think that there's a lot more of it to be explored, and I don't object to it per se. I only object to it when they get away from the music. I see a lot more glamour happening in music and I'm not sorry to see it come, although I probably won't be part of it because my main focus is music. I think because of Bette Midler and the Pointer Sisters and the forties music coming back, which I find myself drifting into too because it feels so good, I think there may be more musicals, a current version of Busby Berkeley. I hope it happens, maybe it will lead to softer music. I wouldn't be surprised if due to the energy crisis things get quieter. I sure hope so. I like acoustic music. But you know the trouble with it is that people have to listen to it, they have to stretch to listen to it, and now people are spoiled because they are used to having it crammed down their ear drums, you didn't have to fight to listen to it.

Fortunately you can still get a beat, maybe that will be enough. Maybe it will become more of a visual thing, but somehow better integrated. I hope I don't get too far away from it because I like all that and I like performing. The thing I don't want to do at this point is get a band back together and try to take it from the bottom up again. The ground has been covered. There are new things to do, new music to play, and I'm anxious to get to it.

*Do you think
glitter rock is just a fad?
Do you think
it will wear itself out?*

CLAUDIA LENNEAR

For someone whose press seems to center on the fact that she looks so good and sings so sexy, the most striking thing about Claudia Lennear is her attitude. She is an extraordinarily positive person. Much of this positivism may stem from the fact that she has had her share of lucky breaks. When she was twenty-one, Ike and Tina Turner found her in Hollywood and asked her to be one of the Ikettes for a tour beginning in Houston, Texas. Her debut on stage followed one four-hour rehearsal.

When Ike and Tina toured with the Rolling Stones in 1969, Claudia began a lasting friendship with Mick Jagger. He wrote two songs for her, and she returned the favor with her own tune, "Not At All," included in her first album for Warner Bros., *Phew.*

Claudia's association with the Turners ended in 1970, and ten days later she found herself on a sound stage at A&M Records where Leon Russell and Joe Cocker were preparing the Mad Dogs and Englishmen tour. A friend, the late Gram Parsons, then a member of the Flying Burrito Brothers, was recording at the studio and invited her down to see what was going on. At first hesitant, Claudia recalls, "I didn't want to go. I didn't have a baby-sitter or whatever and I just went down there and Gram introduced me." The meeting resulted in Claudia's joining the Cocker group and traveling with them for two months. During that time, she was allowed the musical and choreographic freedom that the tight steps and written-out singing parts had denied her with the Ikettes. Labeled the "Stellar Gypsy" by the members of the tour, she would skip across the stage, tambourine in hand, wailing up a storm. She was one of the two women on the tour who were given solo numbers (the other was Rita Coolidge), and much of Claudia's rock identification stems from her rendition of Paul McCartney's "Let It Be," and her active participation in Mad Dogs' music.

With the end of the Cocker tour, Claudia continued recording and traveling with Leon Russell and the Shelter People. She also appeared on the soundtrack for the film *Klute*, and on albums by Hoyt Axton, Delaney and Bonnie, Joe Cocker, Al Kooper, Dave Mason, Nigel Olsson, Humble Pie, Leon Russell, Boz Scaggs, and Stephen Stills, making her mark as an accomplished and sought-after vocalist.

In 1972, Claudia was signed to Warner Bros. Records as a solo artist, and *Phew* was released in early 1973. It was a critical success on some fronts, but genuinely disappointing overall. Claudia is the first to admit it, and gently reminds those who are interested that they might as well forget the whole thing.

The problems with the first album were mainly production problems, too much chaotic noise, and not enough direction. It also tried to be all things to all people, one side having a rock orientation, the other rhythm and blues. As a result, Claudia is deprived of a strong musical identity. Confusion naturally exists due to the fact that black women are ordinarily thought of as soul singers, but Claudia has a rock audience. The problem is not an insurmountable one, as audiences continue to broaden in both areas.

As far as Claudia's personal optimism goes, it seems deep-seated and unshakable. She is not particularly introspective and has the tendency to let matters slide to avoid direct confrontations and emotional turmoil. She is also a person of extremes, and most generalizations can at any given moment, be contradicted.

She is easy to like because of her good nature and straightforwardness. Claudia Lennear's outspoken cheerfulness is refreshing, her musical star is on the rise, and she is ready for hit records and happy times.

I worked with a local Los Angeles band when I was just getting started. We were lucky if we worked once a month. It didn't seem like that big of a thing at the time. I even forget what the name was, but I think it was something like the Superbs. All we seemed to do was practice a lot.

A mutual friend told me about an opening with the Ikettes. You know they have a very quick turnover in personnel, and it's not a hard job to get. There are a lot of former Ikettes around. Working for Ike Turner is like working for any boss. It depends on how much you take and how much you give. He is pretty stern, but everybody knows that story.

When I was with the Ikettes we played the Chitlin Circuit, bowling alleys and bars. Real dives. Not your finest places. We went on tour in the South and it was a real change for me. I was born in Rhode Island and I had never been to the South. It was an education in a sense. A lot of the time, it was awful.

I had gone to college, leaning toward the old standard. Go to college, get that job, although it wasn't going to be anything really special. I thought I might want to teach languages or be an interpreter, similar to the kind they have at the United Nations. Languages were my best subjects. So I ended up singing rock and roll. How do you figure that out?

I always liked music, but I never really thought of it as a career. It just happened. I think I went to a club one night and saw some group that was playing there. I didn't like what they were doing.

What kind of
musical experience did you have
before you joined the Ikettes?

Claudia Lennear / 83

You know how it always looks so easy when you're in the audience, so I thought, I can do that. At the beginning I was pretty much into rhythm and blues because that was what I was around the most. But now if you look at my record collection, it's just one big extreme, just like me. I listen to everything. And my music isn't just rhythm and blues. It's rock, too.

Do you think you had to work harder to establish yourself because you are a woman?

I believe that everybody gets a turn, everybody gets a chance. I don't think that I had to hustle harder because I'm a chick. Everybody's life is planned for them. When your chance comes you just have to be ready for it. There are a lot of chicks who get laid by the director and still don't get the part. There's no guarantee. I don't really think about working around men all the time. Maybe I should stop and think about it more. I'm just kind of trusting.

How do you feel about recording?

Making records can be fun if the people you are working with are good. But it's very difficult. I think if the public had any idea of what went into making those records, they wouldn't bitch about the money they have to pay for them, the $5,98 or whatever it costs now.

It just takes months to make a record. I wasn't happy with my first album at all. I just knew that I wasn't being guided properly and what I felt about it wasn't being taken into consideration. I was having a hard time being heard. Words are really hard to work with. It's too bad you can't just reduce it all to music. Use the music as a language so words wouldn't get in the way and be misunderstood. I can't complain about the record company, though, they've been really good to me.

How do you feel about writing your own material?

I like to write, but I'm not terribly prolific. Probably because instead of just writing down ideas and things, I'm sitting around waiting for this big thing to happen, the Great Idea. Meanwhile, so many great things have already passed by.

Part of the problem is that I don't think. All I ever do is react. If I took the time to think all these things out, it would really drain me, whereas for someone else, it might work really well. It's the same with performing. I just get up there and do it. If you have to psyche yourself up for music, I think there's something basically wrong. Music to me is just energy plus. Before I go on stage, I do get a little nervous, just until about the middle of the first song, but then I'm OK.

84 / Claudia Lennear

About the only people I've ever seen who can overcome a mood and hop up on stage are Tina Turner and Joe Cocker. Tina is always the same. I've seen her crying before she went on stage and then, five minutes later, she'd be up there working. She'd really psyche herself up.

Do you feel
you have to be sexy on stage?

Again, I don't think about it in those terms. I think about being a woman. Every woman wants to look nice, both for herself and to please that certain man. But I don't think I go out of my way. I guess in a sense, I'm trying to get myself off on stage, because you have to do that before you can reach an audience. Maybe that sounds kind of selfish, but I think it's true, at least it is in my case. Also, an audience can tell if you are really enjoying it. They know if you like what you're doing.

How do you feel
about writers and reviewers?

A lot of them are assholes, but then a lot of people in rock and roll are assholes. Writers affect me to the point where I think a lot of them are jerks. I like writers who are forward, who say what they think and who are not kissing anybody's ass. I love honesty, and if they don't like something, they say so. It's silly to me when writers put something down on paper just to please the people they write about or just to go along with what's happening.

I don't have time to worry about the kind of stuff writers are doing, like if they're creating some kind of image for me. It's really worthless to me to fuss over it. I'd rather spend my time writing a song or something meaningful to me, rather than worry about somebody else's problem.

How do you think
being in rock and roll has affected
your personal life?

I don't think it has affected my personal life very much at all. I suppose it could, but I don't think it has. There are always some people who are trying to do you favors for their own reasons, to make themselves look good. They do things at your expense, personally. But so what? I think that's sick and I try not to let it get to me.

A lot of the men I hang out with are musicians, because they are the people I am around the most. But I know a lot of men who aren't in the music business, and it doesn't seem to matter that much. As far as motives are concerned, what does any man want? I mean, what do you want when you go out with a guy? As to the fame and fortune business, I'm not giving up any of it. And I'm not thinking of anybody's bank book when I go out.

Do you think
rock and roll is a lonely business?

Rock and roll lonely? NO! Not with so many of us. There's too many of us, do you hear me, too many. I wish there weren't so many. If it is lonesome, if some people think it is, then those people are probably just loners anyway. People get involved with exactly what they want to be involved with. The ones who say that rock and roll is a sad story are sad stories themselves. It's not the fault of rock and roll. You create your own happiness.

I really try to be as straight with myself as I possibly can. I'm a person of extremes, but I'm extreme enough to the point where I'm still consistently extreme. I'll take a week and go on a binge and get so crazy I'm like a dingbat. The next week I'm just as straight as I was crazy the week before.

I have a few very close friends, I have maybe three close friends, because I'm not that open to a lot of things. I haven't lost any of my privacy because of that fact, and because of the fact that when I am home, I'm almost always at home. I don't go out that much.

How do you feel
about traveling, being on the road?

I love it. The best times in the world are on the road. I love to travel. The main reason it gets hard on you is that you're taking too much shit. That's how it gets hard. You're taking ups and stuff and you get so deranged. That's what makes it tough on you. If you can just manage to keep your health up, it's all right.

I've been doing more concerts lately. Clubs are much more intimate places, but the type of act I am, the music I do, I like concerts better. I prefer being in a bigger place. A David Bowie type of performer is good in a smaller, more intimate atmosphere. He does so many facial things, it's impossible for somebody in the back of a big arena to see. They're going to miss it, all they see is a little dot standing on stage. If you're just skipping across the stage and dancing though, the bigger places are all right.

I travel with a group and I am the one who chooses the musicians. I try to work with them and I want them to feel they're working with me, not for me. That could create a real conflict right there. It make me feel uncomfortable being one chick and having eight guys I have to boss around. I don't like that very much and I'm sure that they feel uncomfortable having a chick boss. So we get together and I go into my little tomboy act and it works out pretty well.

Is your career important to you?

Of course, my God! What a waste of time if it wasn't really important to me. I don't think I have to give up anything for it either. I don't feel any great sacrifices. It's my choice. You do the same thing if you want to be a doctor. One thing I do want to do is get into movies more. I did a small part in a Clint Eastwood movie,

Thunderbolt and Lightfoot. It was such a different thing for me to try to do. I played a secretary. It was a small part, and I worked a few days, but it was really tiring. We worked twelve-hour days. The scene that I did was with Clint Eastwod. I got immediate lockjaw.

Technically, working in movies is different from rock and roll, but basically they have a lot in common. You still kind of have to act on stage when you're singing. It is a performance. In films though, you have to stand on that "X" they make to mark your place, and you can't move. You feel like stretching or moving but you can't get out of focus of that camera. It's very inhibiting.

I think of music as work, but I just try to have fun with it. The audience can make me feel like I'm working. If I can't get to an audience, then I think it's really hard work. It makes me wonder if I'm doing the right thing. It makes me wonder what my purpose is. Then you go to another city and the audience is really good, and you snap out of it.

How do you feel about the traditional role of women in this country?

I think about the two kids and the two cars. But not for long. Ugh! What a bore to have to look at that same face every day. I don't think it's for me. But I do have a seven-year-old daughter. She takes life day by day, just like I do. I don't know it that's good or bad, but there's not much I can do about it. I'll have to say this, if I had it to do over again, if I could be 100 percent sure I'd get Dana, I'd do it. I think it's about the hippest mistake I ever made. She's a wonderful kid.

I truly believe that nobody can make me do anything I don't want to do myself. I'm really stubborn about that. It's probably the only good Taurus trait I have. I really stick to my guns. So whatever I do, I only blame me. That's one of the reasons I haven't had that much experience with drugs. I've never taken acid or any of that stuff mainly because I always thought that I was crazy enough. I don't need any help.

What about your work gives you the most pleasure?

Probably applause. That's a really good feeling to know that you worked and that you really pleased someone. If you think about it, when people go to concerts, it's maybe an hour or two or three out of their lives. If you can make them forget all about everything except that little bit of space in their lives, I really think that's an accomplishment. It's just a good feeling. You might be all sweaty and drained when you come off that stage, but way down underneath it all, not even that far down, you just want to say, "All right!" It's a good feeling.

I think I'm basically a happy person. But like I said I get on those binges. When I'm not happy, I'm really unhappy. I'm very moody. But I'm hardly ever down, and I really kind of fear when that depression is going to come because I can't cope with myself and I have to lock myself in my room, go through those kinds of changes. But as soon as it's over, a day or however long it is, I'm back at it again. I'm just grinning from ear to ear.

Being a woman in rock and roll is probably hard for certain people. Everybody can't be the same way. It's like in a classroom. There's only going to be so many "A" students.

MARIA MULDAUR

Her name is Maria Grazia Rosa Domenica D'Amato Muldaur and she grew up in New York's Greenwich Village during the boom years of folk and bluegrass, when there was music in the streets. The music scene was in the process of growth and experimentation. Washington Square was a focal meeting place for new and untried talent, and coffee houses, clubs, and bars were open to the new trends. The atmosphere was contagious. At Hunter High, a New York school for intellectually gifted girls, Maria helped form a singing group called the Cashmeres.

"We wore long ponytails and matching outfits and we used to cut class and sing in the bathroom," she remembers. "I wrote about eighteen songs which I can only remember fragments of now. We used to go around to the Brill Building and look up publishers' offices and go up the elevator and sing to these guys behind their desks."

These early experiences led to her first disappointments with the vagaries of the music business. "We actually ran into a manager who was lurking in the hallway and he got us a rehearsal studio, some backup work for Jerry Butler, and a deal with Gone Records. All the mothers had to come down to sign contracts because we were all under age. I was sixteen. My mother came screaming into the studio. She insisted that she wasn't going to let *her* daughter become a white slave, and that was it. Good-bye the whole scene."

After she graduated from high school, Maria, who had learned to play fiddle from Gaither Carlton, a traditional bluegrass fiddler and father-in-law of Doc Watson the famous blind flatpicking guitarist, sang and played at parties and hoot nights at Gerde's Folk City, a club in the Village.

The summer Maria turned twenty-one, blues singer Victoria Spivey put together a group to do a jugband record for her label. The Even Dozen Jug Band included Maria, John Sebastian, Steve Katz, Stephan Grossman, Josh Rifkin, and David Grissman. "Then Elektra Records heard that Vanguard Records had signed the Kweskin Jug Band, and they thought jug band music would sweep the nation. So they bought us from Spivey," Maria remembers. "We cut an album in two days, made $65 each, and thought it was hot bananas."

They did two concerts at Carnegie Hall, a Hootenanny TV show and then disbanded. Maria moved to Cambridge and married Geoff Muldaur, whom she'd met when the Kweskin band played the Bitter End in New York. A few months later a vacancy appeared in the

Kweskin group and Maria was asked to fill the gap. She soon became pregnant, but toured right through her seventh month and started again three weeks after her daughter was born.

"The Kweskin band was like a big family. It was a real democracy with everyone getting equal say and those were some real happy, good times. We were a bunch of characters on stage interacting with each other. It was just the carryings-on of a group of friends. I guess people liked that. I did."

The Kweskin Band carried on for six years and when it finally ended, Geoff and Maria settled in Cambridge and then Woodstock. They made two albums for Warner's, "Pottery Pie," and "Sweet Potatoes," with neither recording faring particularly well. About this time Geoff and Maria decided to go their separate ways following nine years of marriage. Maria continued to perform as a solo, and released her first individual effort, *Maria Muldaur*, for Warners in 1973.

Perhaps Maria's most distinguishable characteristic is her spirit. She presents a strong, positive image, usually without sacrificing a certain softness and vulnerability. She is as dedicated to her daughter Jenny as she is to her music, combining the roles of mother and performer with seemingly effortless ease.

Although she lives a carefree rock and roll life-style, Maria's music is not straight rock. Her repertoire includes country and western material, white mountain music, a bit of jazz and Dixieland, some pop, and of course, the legacy of her jug band days. Her voice has an immediately identifiable quality, combining sharpness with ballad warmth. Stylistically, she seems intent on embellishment, rarely holding a note for any specified length when it can be stretched or slightly altered. It is a sometimes unpredictable, consistently appealing trait.

Her stage presence is confident, her movements sexy, and, with a fresh flower pinned into her thick black hair, her manner conveys a gypsylike image. She is slender and graceful, the focus of attention from her sidemen, giving musical keys and enthusiastic glances of encouragement for individual contributions. Her eyes are huge and faunlike, but she is not reluctant to assert herself. This confidence is sometimes accompanied by a kind of toughness, a hard edge which seems to contradict Maria's personal attitudes. On stage she can seem inaccessible and testy, qualities that do not especially please her. She is, however, a person whom other musicians continually like to refer to as a friend, and she is close to several other women in the music business, among the Bonnie Raitt, Wendy Waldman, and Linda Ronstadt.

For Maria Muldaur, 1973 was a coming out year, a time for people to reacquaint themselves with stunning solos such as "I'm A Woman" from the Jug Band days, for a fresh spotlight, an independence, and an industrywide enthusiasm for her huge talent.

I was on the music scene in the Village, and there were things happening every night, parties and concerts, a lot of exciting new music to hear. I was very turned on by country music and by blues. There was a lot of country music in the Village, what later became known as "jewgrass" music. Every Sunday, there would just be dozens of Scruggs pickers. It was just like a revolving Hootenany in Washington Square. You walked around the fountain and there was just every possible kind of music.

I was sort of into it socially and going to college. The Even Dozen Jug Band was forming and they were excited because they were making an album. First it was for Victoria Spivey, then Elektra bought them out. They wanted to have a girl sing a couple of tunes, so they asked me and I said fine.

I also had a friend named Annie Bird who was from Virginia. She was great country flat picker and she knew every Carter Family song. We were really into doing Carter Family stuff, and we would sing at basket houses, we didn't get any salary but the basket was passed around for money. So I was doing that, and then I remember having a group with David Grissman, and Steve Mendel who is now in Deliverance, and Steve Arkin and Fred Weiss, who was with Goose Creek Symphony for a long time playing behind Bobbie Gentry. We were called Maria and the Washington Square

Ramblers, and we worked in a sleazy bar in Long Island, and we each made $15 a night, which was big bananas in those days.

I would happen into these situations. I got involved with the Even Dozen thing, but it didn't look like we were going to get much work. Our first two gigs were at Carnegie Hall, and that was great, but there was no money to hire thirteen people.

Meanwhile, I was getting into the Kweskin Jug Band. Geoff's voice had a revelation-like effect on my consciousness of music. It was so expressive, and I had never heard a white person sing like that.

The closest thing to a decision about music was made when I was going to Hunter College. I'd been sort of sliding along for a couple of years taking what I wanted. I had just started another term, it was September, and they were starting to notice that I had sort of neglected some required courses, things like calculus. So I had an appointment to see the dean. I got up that morning and I had terrible cramps. My appointment was for 2:00. I took lots of Excedrin, I sat in a hot tub, I drank lots of sherry until I was totally blasted.

The appointment came and went and I was sitting around the house picking "I'm A Woman" on the guitar. I taught myself the chords and really got into it. I got happier and happier and all of a sudden I had this flash, this is what I want to do! Fuck college. I wrote the guy I was living with at the time a note saying sorry the house is a mess, but I'll have plenty of time to clean it because I'm not going to school anymore.

That same night I saw Geoff at a party. By that time I was totally loaded, it was the drunkest I've ever been. It's a whole famous episode. I came up to him and lurched at him and said, "I'm going to be you when I grow up." I just felt musically inspired.

Where did you find "I'm A Woman"?

It was the B side of a Peggy Lee single that was on a jukebox in someplace like the Dugout in the Village. I had played it by accident, and it became my favorite song. I would play it fifty times and try to get the words off the jukebox.

Shortly after that, I got involved with Geoffrey and moved to Cambridge. I was really involved with being his old lady, and I really didn't think of singing professionally. A few months passed by and one of the members of the Jug Band left, and they came to me and asked me to join them. I rehearsed twice with them and then learned everything else just from doing it.

How did you feel about going out on your own, making your own album?

I was very apprehensive. I just took it one day at a time. It was already in the works, really. Warner Brothers thought it would be a nice idea for me to make an album. I know that it was also in the works that I was probably breaking up with Geoff at the time when the concept of doing my album came up. So I know that I could eventually do it. But I didn't feel ready to do it at first.

I had gotten some offers in the area where I lived. I did a wild Women Don't Worry workshop at the Philly Folk Festival, and a couple of other things. They were the very first things I did on my own. I had David Nichtern on guitar and Freebo playing bass backing me up.

In the last year of my marriage, we didn't have any gigs, so I was doing any backup work I could find. Artie and Happy Traum were working at the Gaslight down in the Village, and they asked me to come down and play fiddle and sing harmony. So just to keep myself musically alive, I went down there. David was also a friend of theirs who was sitting in. On the third night of the gig, they asked me to sing a solo. I heard David play in back of me, and I really liked the way he played. About a year later, I was doing some gigs and I called him. He needed work and so we got together. We went and did little coffee house jobs.

I remember driving to my first coffee house gig which was at Amherst College. It was my very first solo gig except for the Philly Folk Festival thing, and I cried all the way up there, and kept sticking my head out the window just trying to stop crying. I was thinking, how am I going to get up on stage and sing? What do I say in-between songs? In the Jug Band I had the luxury of not having to worry about any of the details of the gig, what the set was going to be, what to say. I could just float up to the microphone and sing. I just didn't know how I was going to manage it.

I got there and Freebo had driven all the way from Boston to play for nothing to back me up. We had no rehearsal, it was all off the cuff. And it was beautiful. Once I got on stage, the music completely healed me and all my misgivings. It was natural and I said what I had to say in-between songs. It was a wonderful evening. I remember it very vividly.

Then from there I did more and more. Bonnie Raitt's manager, Dick Waterman, kind of got me some work around the northeast. I did a couple of gigs with Bonnie which were wonderful evenings of music. Then I decided not to spend the winter in Woodstock pining away and shlepping to gigs in the snow. So I came to Los Angeles to try to make the record.

I was very scared, though. I thought, how am I going to put this over on Warner Bros.? I had to meet with Lenny Waronker, who was going to produce the album, and I thought he was a great producer. I really respected his work. I had to present myself as if I really knew what I was doing, and I didn't. But it all worked out.

I've been very lucky in that people have come to help me. I felt very unlike Bonnie, who knows exactly what guitar breaks she wants in which place. And she is also able to back herself up on the guitar, so she can really shape the music as she does it. She has more musical knowledge, so I felt like I had to put myself in the hands of other musicians. I'd always done that. I'd always been in a musical family situation with the Jug Band and then with Geoff and the other people we played with. The right people gravitated together to where I didn't even question what they played, it just always worked out. They'd play something nice and I'd sing. I was lucky to have that kind of help on the record, too.

Do you feel as though you have to sacrifice any of your femininity in your work?

I have just recently been going through that. I went through making the album and it was still in an embryonic stage because I was under the wing of my producer, and Warner Bros. was kind of paying for my existence while I was making the album. Stage Two was going out and gigging after the album was finished. I did a few gigs in the summer. It kind of was moving along at a pace I was used to, that I had been used to in the Jug Band. Then all of a sudden the album came out, and everybody really liked it. There were interviews and lots of gigs, and I thought, whew! I can't handle this. It's going much faster than I was used to.

David Nichtern, who has really been like a brother to me, supportive but never coddling, always pushing me back on my own two feet, said, "You're going to have to learn to be a man in this next year." And it's absolutely true. In the sense that—just the way I was brought up, for as old as I am and the kind of background I had, and what my experience had been—a man always handled all the business details and all the major musical decisions. When the Jug Band had a business discussion, I was all too happy to go in the other room and make a cup of tea. I didn't want to hear about percentages. Now I can't do that.

It all is in conjunction with the fact that I am suddenly without a man after ten years. Whatever I would be doing, I would have to be making a lot of major decisions.

Somebody who knows me very well saw me at the concert I did with Loggins & Messina, and said that I had changed, that I had gotten tough. My self-image, until about a year ago, had been, "Oh little me, how am I ever going to do this?" While I was making the record, I worked really hard to stop that. I had to completely change that attitude in myself if I was going to make it.

The concert my friend saw was kind of unusual in the sense that ten minutes before I went on, I found out that my mother's helper and Jenny and another girl had been in a horrible accident in Arkansas. They were driving out here from the East. I knew that my daughter was OK, but I knew that my mother's helper was badly hurt and that my car was wrecked. It was a very shaky thing to hear right before a big concert which I wasn't mad about doing anyway, opening up for a really popular pop act in a huge auditorium in Los

Angeles. I feel I am a much more intimate type of performer, and yet people had said that it would be very good for me, a good introduction to LA.

So that just shows, I guess, how tough I've become, that I went out and did a show that most people thought was great. But someone who really knew me noticed that I had a tough veneer, which is what I was using to hold myself together. A couple of other people have noticed that, and I really don't want that to happen.

I feel like I have probably been overcompensating for having to make bigger and bigger decisions. My life now includes a cast of thousands, mother's helpers, road managers, a band, a business manager, producers, a personal manager. It's a big trip for a folkie who was just going along singing at coffee houses.

I feel like this year has been really good, because I've really gotten strong. I know I can do all kinds of things I never dreamed I could do, and I've felt really good about that. Now that things are finally set up right for me, I feel like I'm with a really good manager, I implicitly trust my producer, I'd like to get back to it, to femininity. For one thing, the main thing is that I'm a mother, and that's the main sacrifice I've made that drives me crazy, trying to do this and do it right and get started so that I'll be set up nicely so that I can take care of my daughter and support her. That's been the toughest part.

I don't know about external femininity, whether I sing soft or hard, but it's difficult having to do that and then come back and try and erase that all out of my mind and just hang out with my daughter without four thousand things happening, and people constantly calling me on the phone. That's been the toughest sacrifice. She's a pretty hip little Aries, she's eight. I talk to her about it and she understands, and it's really hard. All of a sudden within a month she no longer had her dad around, but her mother all of a sudden was taking off all the time to do gigs.

Finally, after a year of trial and error, I have a wonderful mother's helper. It's so strange. I'm in the position of needing an "old lady." All the things I did for my husband for free, I need to pay someone to do. And it can't just be a teenage noonoo who keeps Jenny from running in traffic and gives her an occasional tuna sandwich, but someone who has a reserve of creative maternal energy to pour into her when I'm gone, or else I feel really bad. Thank God I have someone who is going to do it. I also try to arrange my life so I don't gig that much. If I wanted to, I could be gigging every day of the year right now, but I've turned down a lot of jobs to make sure I have enough time to spend with Jenny.

Yes, I do, but it's been hard. I feel like I have a good co-pilot in David Nichtern. Musically, he leads the group. At rehearsal, I can't

Do you feel as though you are the leader of your group?

Maria Muldaur / 97

say, go to this chord or that chord, so he does all that. But I'm getting stronger and stronger about saying things like no, that's a wimpy introduction. I'm more and more able to express, in my own strange way, what I want. I don't have a musical vocabulary, but I can get it out of them. I used to be very timid about what I wanted.

The biggest frustration is finding a good band. I don't just want to be a chick singer with a nebulous backup band. I'm used to a musical partnership of people of something like equal energies, and equal projection on stage. That's what I'm still searching for. I feel like I've found some of the players. Stylistically, there is so much old music that I love. I'm looking for players who can do old, really funky blues, and not just imitate it, but people who have made it a part of themselves, like Ry Cooder and Taj Mahal. It wouldn't be a backup situation; it would be me and them singing and playing and presenting this music. I would like to find stronger entities to work in combination with, and not just be the chanteuse. All these styles are within me, and I would like to find players who have those same styles within them, and we could all say something together.

I think I'm pretty versatile. I do old blues, I do jazz, I do country, I do a little rock, and I pull most of it off OK. That makes it somewhat diverse, but it would be even more diverse if there were different voices. I want a band that's versatile, players who can sing harmony. I have a piano player, Jeff Gutcheon, who can do all those styles, and a guitar player who pretty much can.

Has it been difficult for you to make your musical preferences known?

In the Jug Band, it was such an equal five-way thing, and I was one of three lead singers. Jim Kweskin or Geoff would usually come up with tunes for me. I would kind of accept it. They were the ones who had walls and walls of old blues albums.

When we left the Jug Band and moved to Woodstock and we were getting ready to do our own second album, suddenly I wanted to do some Eric Kaz tunes. He brought me some new things fresh off the presses, and I loved them and they were just right for my voice. I wanted to start singing more than just "Rich Land Woman Blues," the old delicate little blues things. I brought the new tunes to the band and it was just like they didn't hear me. That's when I started really getting frustrated. It was very clearly Geoff's band. I thought it was very unfair. That particular bunch of guys didn't give me much help in that way.

However, now that this is my trip, they'll do it. I'm the singer.

Your own musical instrument seems to be the fiddle. Where did you pick that up?

I play the fiddle a little bit, in fact less than I used to. I have not had time lately to do it. I don't have the luxury of sitting around and practicing. I picked it up over ten years ago when I first heard Doc

Watson. His father-in-law, Gaither Carlton came up to New York and did a concert, and I just flipped out, and became Gaither Carlton's groupie. He was sixty-five at the time. We went down to North Carolina and visited them, and he taught me how to play the fiddle. I didn't even play in regular tuning until about a year ago. It was all by ear.

I can play pretty simple country and Cajun stuff pretty well, but it's not a backup instrument. I can't set the groove on my fiddle, so it's kind of incidental, it's not like playing piano or guitar or even bass.

Do you think you would like to work into playing piano or guitar?

I don't think my great aptitude will ever be playing an instrument. I finally have a nice little guitar that I can play, and I plan to take lessons as this scene smooths itself out. I do want to learn to play, and get a little picking together. Also, in the process I want to learn what the chords are, all that simple stuff so I will be able to communicate a little better with my fellow musicians.

Do you feel like you have to be sexy on stage?

I think I probably used to. I never thought much about it. I just got up on stage, and I normally love to dance, I just love to boogie around. If the music moves me, I dance. So I kind of did that on stage, and I put a certain amount of body English into my music, and that's what I considered it. It helps me get the music out.

I like to look as nice as I would look if I were going out to have a drink or something. I don't go through any huge number with fancy clothes, but I try to look sort of foxy, rather than frumpy, but just sort of funky and comfortable, too. And I am finding a change. I've done "Don't You Feel My Leg" a whole lot, because it's always the big request, and I've always done "I'm A Woman," and that had a certain sex appeal to it, but "Don't You Feel My Leg" is even more sort of camp-vamp. I do a whole little number with it, because it would be really dumb to stand there like a clodhopper and sing that song. But I'm getting kind of weary of it.

I recently started thinking, what if I went to a club like the Troubadour in LA wearing my hiking boots and a baggy pair of pants and a sweatshirt? Would they like me for my music? I don't know what I'll do. I still like to look nice, I can't help it. But maybe that side of it will wear down a little.

How is the music business affecting your personal life?

Right now, it's not giving me much time. I've never been known for my self-discipline in the first place, so it all runs away with me. I'm getting more forceful. I'm learning how to say no.

Also, of course, there are no groupies for girls. So you're out there on the road, and it's such a ludicrous situation. People are drooling over you in the audience, but where is one guy who will come in afterwards who isn't just a teenager with his tongue hanging out? Just a nice dude in the town who'll take you for a cup of coffee. It's just a completely ridiculous situation most of the time when you're on the road.

Also, I think it's very threatening to a lot of guys to see a woman with her own scene together. She isn't going to just want to pack up her sleeping bag and wander off with him, not to mention that I have a daughter. So I think if I find someone I want to spend a whole lot of time with, it'll have to someone who is as secure in what he's doing as I am in what I'm doing, and getting off on it. Not even necessarily commercially successful, but someone who just has a good sense of himself and believes in what he's doing, and feels he's on the right track, and isn't threatened by a woman who's making it in this realm.

Do you feel like
you have a good sense of yourself?
Do you feel
musically confident and secure?

More and more. This whole experience has done it. Even if the whole record industry were to go out the window tomorrow, and I had to go back to Woodstock and wait on tables, it has taught me confidence, it's made me strong.

Sometimes I get discouraged. I hear someone like Bonnie sing or Aretha Franklin or Ann Peebles, strong, great voices, and I think, what am I trying to do? But I know that I have developed a style, and that my singing has gotten four times as strong as it was a year ago. Just my vocal power. I never thought I could more than just sweetly croon along. I am getting a better sense of what I want to do, and how I want the music around me to be made.

Do you think
writers and reviewers have
made an image for you?

A lot of them are guys, and a lot of them think I'm, well, sexy. I say it apologetically. I shouldn't aplogize for it. I can't deny that it's been very good, the fact that I don't have a big hook nose and lots of zits must help a lot. Your physical projection helps people like you or not like you. I feel after thinking it over a lot, and going through a lot of changes, that I don't have to apologize.

Actually, I thought I was going to get a lot of flack from "I'm A Woman" and songs like that. But I feel that basically it's a song about positive, female self-reliance. It lauds a lot of traditional female roles, but it says I can do all this stuff, I can grease the car, powder my face, go out and boogie. It also lauds the healing power of women, of womanly love. I put it in mothballs for years, but it remains a really right-on song on a whole different level now that

Maria Muldaur / 101

I'm doing it again. I kind of had to reexamine it when I started gigging a lot.

I don't want to be made a sex object, but I don't mind because that's part of who I am. I am a woman and I do want to boogie and I do want to relate to men from a sexual part of my nature. I do gospel tunes, too, I do tunes which have nothing to do with that. And I do tunes that I picked long ago before there was any female consciousness, like "Rich Land Woman Blues," that I musically related to, that are vampy and alluring.

I don't want to become any more of a sex symbol or whatever it is that people think I am right now. That's why I starting fantasizing about wearing hiking boots and stuff on stage. I don't want to be put in this sexy outfit that I get locked into and can't get out of.

It's kind of the opposite of what Alice Stuart has said. Now that she's really been straight on and established herself as a musician, she's thinking about her feminine appeal. Now that I seem to have established my feminine appeal, I want to get more down to the presenting of the music.

Do you think you're the same person off stage that you are on stage?

Basically. In a concert situation, I feel a little more pressured and I don't rap at the audience as naturally. But when I'm in a club, I just say whatever comes off the top of my head and just joke around. It's nice having David to be silly with on stage.

Sometimes, once in a while, if I feel something really serious that has nothing to do with entertainment that I want to tell the audience, I do. I dance when I feel like dancing. It's not like I have a routine that I go out on stage and do, although you can get trapped into that, especially in a concert when you're the opening act, and you know the audience didn't really come to see you, and you've got forty-five minutes to do the best you can. You really don't have the time to just lay back and be more natural, although I feel like I'm going to bust through that and do it anyway.

I try to be the same person off stage. I want to narrow that gap as much as possible. Otherwise you get trapped in your own puppet show. When you're out there in front of people, you should show them who you are. A flashy act is like an incredible cartoon that you can watch a few times and be dazzled by, but if the music isn't there, who cares? Even sometimes if the music is there, you get weary, it wears you out. And it gets in the way of the music.

Are you basically a positive person?

I'm learning to be. I was raised a Catholic, and I shed that pretty early in life. I went through this long marriage, nine years, and I had been married before that, so I had put in a total of twelve years of monogamy, from the time I was eighteen to the time I was thirty.

This was my first year as a single girl. It's a funny place to start, with a kid and with all this other stuff to do. I didn't know, after being married that long, how to relate to people as a single woman. I'm getting better at it all the time, but of course anything new is hard.

Just in this year, by going through all these things, and saying I'm not going to be able to do it, I'm not going to be able to do it, and then with the support of friends saying I think I can, I think I can, and then doing it, it's completely changed me. For the first time this year, I have lots of days of being happy and unburdened. I'm still being hassled to death, but I'm now basically positive.

I don't think I'm self-destructive. For a while I was drinking a lot and music was my only solace, the only space in which I felt whole. But I'm not on a rock and roll self-destruct trip at all. I've got Jenny first of all, and I'm basically not that kind of person. It's just nice in this last year, to notice—gee, I'm not miserable today. At first I sort of felt something was wrong, something was missing, and it was that basic feeling of misery, that sort of daily nagging. When it started going away I almost felt guilty that I was feeling so good, but it's getting better all the time.

Has the woman's movement influenced your thinking in any way?

I've never gotten heavily involved in it. While I was in the Jug Band, I earned the same money as Geoff, I worked all the same hours, went to all the same rehearsals, did all the baby care, every bit of it, all the laundry, cooking, cleaning. I did everything he was doing, plus all the traditional women's things. And I kept feeling, this is lopsided, this is not right. I would make these feeble protestations, but it never would get itself together. I'm not putting the blame on anybody. That's how he was raised, and that's how I was raised, and that's how everybody around us was raised.

Then I read a great pamphlet called *The Politics of Housework.* It was very wittily written about how you bring up the new consciousness of sharing the housework, and how he says, "You're right, darling, that sounds right on," and how he gets out of it. It was so perfect, and I read that and then read it to Geoff and, although be balked at first, he did agree to start making some small concessions towards helping out with stuff in the house.

If I had to think of one main influence the women's movement had, that was it. It did change things. Although once we moved to the country where there was a lot of heavy outdoor work to do with the house we got, I was happy to be just fixing dinner while the guys were lugging huge stones and chopping down trees. It was a fine division of labor as far as I was concerned.

It's affected me in a lot of ways, like making me wonder if I am a sexual object, and giving me strength to feel that I'm not completely lost if there isn't a man at the helm of my life.

One thing I don't like about the women's movement is that they

Maria Muldaur / 103

make sex such a political issue. It's hard enough as it is to honestly relate sexually to somebody in every ramification, and I don't just mean in bed, but where they're coming from, where you're coming from, what they want of you. I feel we need all the friendship between the sexes as we can get, and I think a lot of women have such a pugilistic militant chip on their shoulders. I can understand why they're angry. Believe me, I could fill your book with a list of grievances of male chauvinist shit that has happened to me, but I just don't see any point in having that angry attitude.

For instance, the exception is that one experience in the Geoff and Maria band, and that was largely because it was my husband who was running the band, and that was also the way our relationship was set up. Outside of that, I have not run into any discrimination because I'm a woman trying to sing music. I've had nothing but real cooperation, and not lecherously, either. Most of the guys I play with just straight on enjoy hearing me sing and want to help me out, and the guys who have been in my band have gently helped me be their leader. I just think that attitude works out best in the end.

It seems that the primary element is that you enjoy being a woman. You don't feel it would have been easier for you if you had been a man?

No, I think men have it much tougher. I really do. They've got so many other pressures that they grow up with, like having to make it. To me, I feel if for some reason I totally flop as a professional singer, it's not going to really affect me. It's going to affect my pocketbook a lot and kind of put me through changes, but it's not going to affect the basic core of who I feel I am on this earth.

I wasn't brought up to think that if I don't make it out there I'm a piece of shit. So I could just go back to being a mother, I could go on welfare and food stamps and take care of Jenny and have some friends and play music at home and not feel like I just didn't cut it out there on this planet.

As I get more involved in the "outside world," I see the luxury a lot of women have had in not having to deal with it. It's worth dealing with if there's something you want to get done. It's a world that was set up by men and a lot of arbitrary shit was laid on them that they considered necessary to really be a man, and that's why the scene is as fucked up as it is.

We're lucky not to have had that hammered into us as children. We may have had a lot of other things, but we're much more in touch with ourselves, and that's why we have developed this consciousness over the past few years.

BONNIE RAITT

Bonnie Raitt is an emotional person in an emotional idiom—a rock and roll lady who prefers the blues. The ability to relate to her lyrics has given her albums a personal quality not often found in the industry, possibly because the feelings are essentially basic, while the lyrics she chooses are essentially poetic. She has exquisite taste in her material which serves in some ways as compensation for her hectic working pace.

An extensive traveler, Bonnie often works in three or four different cities in one week, but the traveling seems to have come naturally to her as her father, John Raitt, spent many years starring in theatrical touring shows. He was the leading man in many Broadway musicals, including *Carousel, Pajama Game,* and *Oklahoma,* and Bonnie spent her early years alternating between New York and Los Angeles.

The East Coast seems to have held an intellectual allure for Bonnie, an attraction that is a carryover from the summers she spent at a Quaker camp, learning, among other things, about blues and folk music and listening to records made by people who would later become her close friends. From her pre-teen years, Bonnie remembers a distaste for the current popular songs, and a strong interest in traditional blues. As a result of her comfort in the East, Bonnie has preferred the Cambridge area of Massachusetts as her residence between jobs, replete with activism and political involvement. Although she now finds the atmosphere of her native Los Angeles somewhat more pleasing, she continues to hold to her chosen causes. Her primary concern involves the plight of many old bluesmen, some of whom taught her now to play her distinctive blend of slide guitar and blues. She finds it inexcusable that men like Mississippi Fred McDowell, Son House, or Arthur Crudup should live their lives in relative obscurity and real poverty while others profit from their songs and techniques. McDowell died in June 1972, and Bonnie's second album is, in part, dedicated to him.

In addition, she often does benefit concerts at colleges with the stipulation that she be allowed to bring along a supporting act. A recent example was her appearance at UCLA with Robert Pete Williams, a bluesman whom most of the students in the audience had never even heard of, let alone seen. It was a rare opportunity to see and hear a classic practitioner of slide guitar.

This emotional identification has come through on her records and predominates on stage. Bonnie has three albums on Warner Bros. The first, recorded on a shoestring in a Minnesota backwoods garage, is titled simply *Bonnie Raitt*. The second is called *Give It Up*, and the third, released in the fall of 1973, is *Takin My Time*. Not unlike her live performances, each record correlates the traditional with the modern, taking consistently excellent examples of each. To old tunes by Sippie Wallace and Fred McDowell, she adds those of fine contemporary writers like Jackson Browne, Joel Zoss, Eric Kaz, and Chris Smither. Her finest work emerges when she abandons the affected blues inflection which seems unnatural to her, and sings in her own straightforward manner. Bonnie, at her most soulful, expresses her own feelings, not some preconceived notion of traditional dictates.

At twenty-four, Bonnie Raitt is an accomplished guitarist and a singer of exceptional quality. She is one of the fortunate few whose work seems more pleasing on repeated hearings. Her music does not overwhelm you; rather, its appeal is often subtle and understated. Its earthy sophistication demands attention and deserves greater audience identification. Bonnie equates politics with music, reducing many complexities to relating to and caring about people. She is reflective, idealistic, and honest—uninhibited and candid.

Performing on stage sitting down, Bonnie is a soft image of cascading red hair and innocent freckles, a contrast to the strength of her vocal delivery. Her voice has a quality of warmth and projects an insight and understanding of her lyrics—lyrics that are not merely words, but situational overviews, highlighted with the proper instrumentation. The almost casual delivery can, however, turn at any moment into a rocking uptempo celebration, the mood altered without the usually jarring sense of loss. Her sets depend very much on her changeable moods. At times, her on-stage banter gets fairly raunchy, a fact that tends to bolster her image, if somewhat unfairly, as a "blues mama," at other times she seems almost morose. Bonnie is not a showperson in that sense. She is real, and her emotions are sometimes painfully visible.

Bonnie Raitt is organized, she is goal-directed, and she takes the days as they come. She doesn't waste her feelings, her words, or her music. She's a lovely rock and roll lady, and her personal cause is the blues.

It stemmed from a liking of soul music, really. I never could get into the beach-party bingo that was junior high school in the early '60s in Los Angeles. I was always drawn to Motown, Memphis, or protest folk music, rather than Jan and Dean, Neil Sedaka, or even good white rock and roll like Buddy Holly. Just personal taste, I guess. Who's to say why one person gets into Sun Ra and another Trini Lopez when they're two seats away in the same algebra class?

I spent my summers from the age of eight to fifteen at a liberal, progressive, co-ed camp in the Adirondacks in New York where the counselors and some kids were already picking up on the burgeoning protest movement and folk music revival. The staff went to schools like Antioch and Swarthmore and I always idolized the most radical ones. My family were Quakers in the Baez-Seeger tradition, and aside from my father making his living in musical comedy and us living in LA, a lot of my orientation as a kid was towards counter culture music, art, and politics. I always wanted to be older, wear black, get my ears pierced, go to the Newport Festival, get arrested—but I was still a squirt.

One way to pretend that I could be older was at least to learn to play the music. It was my way of showing my California friends that everything wasn't like *American Graffiti* after all. I started teaching myself guitar off John Hammond, John Hurt, Joan Baez, John Koerner records when I was about eleven or so, and gradually it became "my thing." As I got to be around fourteen, I could actually go to demonstrations and pierce my ears, so protest and folk music as a substitute were pushed to the wayside, becoming a bit passé in my fickle pubescent head. After all, I had gone through all that as a "younger woman" and, now that even my California friends were picking up on it, I had to find something different with which to assert my nonconformity.

Adolescent hangups aside, I still found myself liking blues and a more soulful brand of folk music than happy-go-lucky singalong stuff with "smile on your brother" kind of messages. To this day, it irks me when reviewers try to say "She's doing less blues, more soul," because to me, Muddy Waters and Smoky Robinson just aren't that different where it counts. Robert Johnson and Sly Stone, Sippie Wallace and Etta James, who cares? They're all saying the same things to me.

And as for my father's music, I think it's great, too. The Pointer Sisters just recorded "Steam Heat" from one of his shows, *Pajama Game.* So would I if I could pull it off. He and I may do a remake of Rufus and Carla Thomas duets. Who knows?

Did your father encourage you?

Not really, although he gets a kick out of the music. My two brothers and I have always been music freaks. Of course we were exposed to his shows and my mother was my father's pianist for years. I took piano lessons for five years, but other than that I just picked the guitar on my own. I used to be in camp and school musicals and play for my friends, but it was more like a hobby than something I took seriously. I learned guitar kind of spastically off of records after school. *Blues at Newport, 1963* was the first real influence, and there were country blues records and John Hammond's first record, especially. He was another young, white interpreter of older styles, plus I had an insatiable crush on him. To this day, all I have to do is see someone with a greasy DA and I drop my picks.

There weren't many guitar players around who played anything more than your standard Travis picking, bluegrass flatpicking, or Dick Dale "Wipe Out" styles. Muddy Waters, John Lee Hooker, Son House, John Hammond, John Koerner, and Dave Ray all played a tougher, more rhythmic kind of style, closed right hand, down the neck, less one note, melodic stuff like B.B. King or T. Bone Walker. I'm playing a big jazz electric guitar now, trying to learn more jazz and soul riffs, Cornell Dupree, Steve Cropper type things.

I must admit I don't practice nearly as much as I used to, less free time, I suppose. I don't like the pressure of having to be so "good for a girl," and even after we laugh at that as a joke, the pressure is still there. Also, I'm lazy.

Were you thinking about doing anything as a career?

Not at all. I moved East and went to a Quaker school in Poughkeepsie, progressive, like that camp, for the last two years of high school. I went to college in Cambridge and lived there from 1967 to 1973. Cambridge has always had a lot going for it in terms of the leftist movement and good music. I'd finally made it to "the East" only by the spring of my freshman year, the Club 47 had closed and the camaraderie I was expecting gave way to a primarily college and rock scene.

By the fall of '68 I had become good friends with Dick Waterman, who was and still is booking nearly all the great bluesmen still living—Son House, Skip James, Mississippi Fred McDowell, Junior Wells, Buddy Guy, Robert Pete Williams, Big Boy Arthur Crudup, J.B. Hutto, Mance Lipscomb, etc. Through Dick, I met and became friends with all those people as well as Muddy Waters, Howlin' Wolf, and just about every artist I'd ever idolized. We all traveled around together whenever someone would have a concert. There were lots of excellent mini-blues festivals going at Beloit, Notre Dame, Howard, and Villanova, as well as the larger Ann Arbor, Philadelphia, and Newport Festivals.

I started hanging around the blues circuit more and more, left school for a while in the spring of '69 and was working for the American Friends Service Committee in Philadelphia. As summer approached, the idea of a day job seemed less and less attractive, so I asked Dick if he could finagle a way for me to play in a small club in Philly called the Second Fret. Since I was hanging out in clubs anyway, I figured it would be great if I could get paid for something I already did as a goof, and be able to sleep late. We managed to pull it off, and I worked there over the summer and continued to play around Boston and Worcester through the next year when I went back to school in Cambridge.

By spring of 1970, I played at Harvard with James Taylor and then at a big club near Philadelphia called the Main Point with none other than my Clearasil crush, John Hammond. Then the Philadelphia Folk Festival invited me to play that summer and from then on I decided to take it up as a career. Luckily, I got a lot of "package-deal" bookings through Dick Waterman where I would open for Fred McDowell or J.B. Hutto or on the tail end of blues festivals where they needed a girl for something different. I think Fred and them got a kick out of seeing someone so much younger and different playing their kind of music, and I couldn't have been happier than traveling and playing with them.

Did they treat you well?

Oh yeah. We're good friends, in a special sort of way. Obviously, there are a lot of gaps—age, race, background, teeth, color—but there was something very poignant about my relationship with Fred, with whom I was the closest, that couldn't be duplicated if it were just a young white girl and an old white man, or two black people of different generations. The fact is, aside from Taj Mahal, Larry Johnson and a handful of others, not many young blacks are into country blues, certainly no one Fred knew. And similarly, aside from jazz musicians, very few older whites are into blues. It's just a special kind of distance that allows for a tremendous amount of respect and warmth to flood back and forth, a kind of pride and sentimentality that rarely exists any more, except among people who share a love for a certain craft and culture.

Since '68, blues people have become among the dearest friends I have, but it's hard to have to accept that some of them are very old and sick and to watch them being ripped off and ignored, a whole musical heritage fading away. I've watched my father, also a man of integrity who doesn't change his style or image to be "hip" with fickle times, get ripped off or passed over by the same pigs in sharkskin who signed away Arthur Crudup's rights to "That's All Right Mama," or burned a Chicago blues band on the road while not daring to do the same to a white band with a powerful record company and agency to back them up. Young or old, white or black, wet head or dry look there are still so many scum promoters around, I couldn't begin to tell you. I'm afraid blues people don't wield too much power in the marketplace.

How did you develop your bottleneck style, with the bottle on your middle finger?

The same spastic way I learned chords backwards off a record player. I had never seen anyone play bottleneck when I was sixteen, so I just guessed. I used to flip the finger a lot, as all good LA punks did, and I guess I got used to isolating that one finger. Of course, when I grew up and saw that everyone else either uses their ring or pinky finger, I laughed a bit, but it was too late to change. I used to sit for hours and play to records and then I got to pick up specific tunings and licks from watching Fred or Son House up close.

Do you think you had to work harder because you're a woman?

No, I think it was easier. There has always been an overload of male singer-songwriters. I know at least three or four in New York, Cambridge, San Francisco, and Los Angeles who can't work because there's already a John Sebastian, Neil Young, James Taylor, Jonathan Edwards, ad infinitum. There's only a certain number of types that can be absorbed by the music business at any one time. If James Taylor is a hit, then record companies will sign on lots of James Taylors. Soon the market is glutted and it's time for a run on Lead Okras. Without a record contract, you can't work for very long, at least not out of the cider and doughnut college coffee house circuit, which is fine if you like cider and doughnuts.

With me, when I finally decided to do music for a living, I probably got those early jobs *because* I was a girl, and also played something a bit different. Most female performers at the time had sweet, small voices and did exclusively folk material. As with booking blues men, a club will have its token female folkie, then its token angry young man, its token blues act, etc. Since there was already Joni Mitchell, Judy Collins, Laura Nyro, Janis Joplin, the only openings were for girls who played something different. I have a relatively sweet and small voice, but I played different songs, a bit more macho guitar and "yeah, that bottleneck—that's a great gimmick, honey—don't lose that." No one was doing quite that mix of material and I had a good contact for jobs through Dick. That, with a few good reviews, and I was in.

Now it's tougher and tougher to break into the business just because of how the economy of the music industry (i.e. America) works. During the prosperous times, everyone is signed up and can record. Once the vinyl supply gives out, people get dropped or not signed. There's a performer filling almost every type of description by now, even groups that parody other groups. The public taste is still deliberately kept at whatever level the industry finds convenient. I don't think there's any way I would have the energy or stomach to put up with the pimping it takes to start out today. I'm very lucky to have had a career dumped in my lap at an easy time.

No, not really. Some clubs are owned or run by women. There are a lot of successful women in the music business—writers, publicists, reviewers, photographers, managers, secretaries—a lot of whom got their jobs because they were women. But the business is as sexist as any other; you must be an *attractive* woman, with all the qualities that befit the mode of the day. The women who succeed have probably always succeeded in what they tried. That doesn't mean society doesn't discriminate by not giving every woman or man an even chance to be "attractive."

Do you feel as though you are constantly working around men?

In terms of my life as a performer, many women want to sit in and think they should be able to just because they are women and I'm into the women's movement. But there are so many people who want to sit in—men and women—that it just isn't fair to let someone in without hearing them first. You owe it to an audience who's paid to see some entertainment, not a contest of who's the most deserving person to sit in. You can't say yes to one and not to another.

I hope that more and more women are getting their own musical outlets together. Now that there are women here and there who are playing tough-ass rock and roll and not feeling held back about being better than a man at writing, playing, reviewing, etc., hopefully things will loosen up a bit. But it's a ways off. People still don't take a band like Fanny seriously. How many albums do they have to put out before the reviewers stop saying, "This album really proves that they're not just a gimmick, it's time to take them seriously as musicians" and then proceed to ignore the music just the same?

Bonnie Raitt / 113

*How do you feel
about making records, aside from the
fact that recording is necessary to be able
to perform in clubs?*

So far, I haven't made a record that didn't totally drain me physically and emotionally. You lose sleep, sanity, your best friends, and any sense of proportion for about two months, when you can finally listen to your own songs without cringing. They shouldn't be as difficult as they are for me, but most women are not in the position of overseeing their own projects. I pick the studio, the producer, the musicians, and the material. Most performers, especially women, are produced, and most producers are men. I can only think of one or two women producers and I don't think they're active at the moment. It's a question of finding the right material and arrangements to fit a particular artist's voice and personality.

I wish I could just dump myself in someone else's hands, but I have a lot of untested, specific ideas about how I want the music to sound and I want the right at least to try those ideas without having to relinquish the final say. Unfortunately, I drive everyone in the studio crazy because I often have to hear a song several ways before it feels right to me and they can't understand why I haven't figured all the arrangements out beforehand. I didn't pick up a band for the road until after my third album, and I'm only now beginning to learn the delicate ways that egos and musical tastes have to be coddled in order for any good music to come out.

A big problem for me is that I tend to hire my friends, liking what they play individually and hoping that they'll get along when we start working on a tune. I've been more interested in combining old styles of music in new ways than in creating a totally unique, personal sound. But the situation can backfire when you have a barrelhouse pianist trying to mesh with a jazz bassist, a Memphis soul drum sound, me on National slide guitar and maybe Freebo in the hall on tuba. I have yet to find the one producer or engineer who can extract what it is I'm aiming at and translate it in the technical and emotional climate most studio musicians are used to.

It's very hard for the guys to accept me being in charge, and yet needing their help to know what I'm getting at. When someone I'm close to isn't playing up to par, I tend to shy away from the problem rather than deal with it, and this of course, alienates the other musicians even more. I'm sure there's a lot of resentment on their part when I'm obviously so vulnerable and yet try to get them to play something different; you know, "Who are you to be telling me what to play when you don't even play this instrument?"

They don't actually say it, but I can certainly understand if they feel it. I get up on a high horse because I feel inadequate at explaining myself and yet I'm afraid they're reacting to me as ineffectual, hysterical, or bitchy. The fear is based on my own personal insecurity I think, rather than any real sexist threat. I'm not afraid of being strong, just of not being liked or respected.

Most of the guys I've worked with are really not sexist. They're usually quite helpful and glad, in fact, to be working with a woman who's trying something a bit more complicated than most. I do have a lot of homework to do musically and as I respect and like myself more, I probably won't be so touchy about what other musicians are thinking, or blaming it on sexist attitudes which don't necessarily apply. Everybody's vulnerable and jumpy in a studio situation. There is a lot of ego-tripping and backbiting. I don't expect making records will ever be as much fun as playing live or jamming, but hopefully it will get easier and not quite so earthshattering.

The problems of being a woman are not so much in the studio or on the road as they are in personal life. I could be the most brilliant producer and performer and I'd still have the same personal problems. There are people who don't like working for a woman, but hopefully I won't be working with them. Luckily I have that control. I can always dump this as a career if it becomes too much of a struggle, but at the moment, there's nothing else I want to do as much, so I'm left with the problems basic to a woman in this life-style.

The biggest problem seems to be that the more successful I get, the unhappier I tend to be. The pressure of being a headline act as opposed to an opener, of having control over my bookings and recording, the financial responsibilities of keeping a band—all are a necessary part of my "coming of age." I'm not complaining so much as longing for the days when I was driving myself and my guitar around to little gigs in New England and feeling on top of the world.

The unhappiness comes more from a growing sense of isolation. I've been traveling so much the last few years that I've lost touch with some of my old friends. I often feel as if they're checking me out each time I see them as to whether I've "gone Hollywood," sold out, or maybe just whether they still know me at all.

The one major obstacle for women in this business is that the more successful you get, the more you tend to intimidate the men around you whom you may want to get next to. It's harder and harder to maintain the relationships I do have, and to break down the barriers enough to start new ones. I'm just lonely a lot of the time. Guys may pick up girls on the road, but I don't know many women who get into that kind of scene. Besides, how can you even meet someone in the chaos of dressing rooms and one-night concerts when you're leaving the next day? Horniness aside, it's the tenderness and being close to someone that I miss and those kinds of relationships are not made overnight. What guy is going to fight his way back to my dressing room? What's he going to say when he gets there? That he really likes me? I mean, everybody says that, "I really liked your show."

Bonnie Raitt / 115

That's one reason that you tend to go out with other musicians, or people involved with radio, journalism, or record companies. They're the only ones you can meet in a relatively un-uptight manner. But it's still no picnic to get to a level of trust. Even if they're hip to the fact that you might be better known by accident or that you think what they're doing is just as important, the difference in success eats away at the most liberated relationships.

A lot of women go out with their managers or with guys in their bands, but no self-respecting guy who isn't involved with your act is going to drop what he's doing and follow you around. Not that I'd want him to anyway.

Sometimes you've been on tour and you've saved up enough money to get the hell out for a while. Most of the time the guy either doesn't have the money to join you or the same time free, and very few guys would be able to accept a woman paying for their vacation. That's what's sad, all those nights on the road, the places and things to do that could be so much more fun if you had someone to share them with. That's why I am trying to get to the point where I can work less, spend more time in a place of my own, getting to know one group of people very well so I won't have to feel so rootless and lonely when I am on the road.

Do you think rock and roll is a sad business?

I think it's show business in general. People seem to be drawn into it who have a greater need of reinforcement, especially of superficial qualities. Their whole sense of self-worth can depend on their looks, current price, and place on the charts. Of course, that's nothing new. It seems that the more brilliant someone is, at least a lot of the artists I consider brilliant, the crazier, more compulsive, and isolated he is. I'd just settle for being mediocre and happy, myself.

I mean, I like traveling and playing, and especially being close to people who just blow me away with their brilliance and how in touch they are with something truly special. That almost makes the craziness worth it. My work used to be an extension of my life. Now I'm afraid it's the other way around. So many hours are spent organizing, traveling, and preparing for a gig, it seems the only peace I get lately is when I finally get up on stage. The number of people who want to talk to you, interview you, play you their songs—no matter how much of your time you give, you're always going to disappoint someone.

There's a lot of self-indulgence that can turn into self-destruction in this business. Most of the people I know have some kind of problem with excess, either drinking too much or doing too much dope. The potential of doing this for a living is remarkable. The fact that you can do something you enjoy, that will give people more insight and pleasure, and getting paid for it is great. But the whole scene makes me a bit sick.

Creativity is great but it's no excuse for the kind of chic decadence and overindulgence in mansions, dope, vanity, and ripping audiences off that a great majority of show business people are into. I'm no saint, but I can't say I'm too excited about the level of political consciousness I see around me. Most of the musicians I know aren't political, and most of the political people I know aren't into expressing themselves artistically. I don't think I could give up either one and be happy, but happy is a ways off anyway right now, so I'll call it a draw.

How do you feel
about writing your own material?

I've written five or six songs. They're on the first two albums. I didn't write any for this last record because I didn't have the time. I write on the piano and there aren't too many in Holiday Inn rooms. I haven't really had my own place to hang out and play music for the last year, but hopefully when I get my house together, I'll get back to it.

I'm not really a writer and don't feel the need to write, any more than I feel a need to practice the guitar. I tend to resent people who pressure me with statements like, "Only when she writes more of her own material will she become a mature artist." I'm not going to be what anyone else wants me to be. If they think it looks good when I stand up and dance around, it almost makes me want to go back and sit down just not to be fitting their fantasy of what would make me effective.

I'm primarily an interpreter of other people's songs, and as long as I keep finding songs that say what I would have wanted to say anyway, I probably won't be writing that much.

Do you feel
you have to be sexy on stage?

No. As a matter of fact, I feel uncomfortable when it seems like the audience is relating to me that way. I play guitar sitting down because that's the way I play, and occasionally I stand up when we're doing a faster, rhythm and blues song. But the way people whistle when that moment in the set comes drives me crazy. I feel like a Kewpie doll or some reincarnation of that Joplin-blues-queen-how-much-do-you-drink? bullshit. If I stand up and boogie around, it's because I feel like boogying around, not because it makes a "better show."

I deliberately mix the set up so that it's the most widespread expression of the moods I feel. There's a kind of manic energy that a crowd will develop when all they want to do is the Eternal Boogie.

I enjoy getting crazy too when I go see someone who brings that out in me, but I myself don't want to be locked into any one image when I'm on stage. Sometimes I'm sad, sometimes funky, but either way, I want to determine what to communicate and when. I'd go nuts if I had to be some wind-up doll doing what I thought the audience wanted most. It's hard enough making your living out of opening yourself up, let alone having it be a mass vivisection.

Labels are a journalist's problem, not mine. They just make me mad or sad for the people who have to reduce a person's work to that level. In terms of good responsible criticism, I'm a great fan of reading everybody's reviews. It's a great art. It's also very important for people to be able to have a standard by which to judge whether to buy an album to go see someone. Smartass putdowns, ego-tripping, or a reviewer who self-admittedly never liked that particular artist or style of music panning a show is just irresponsible and a waste of time.

I'm my own harshest critic so whenever a review hits the nail on the head, I'm pleased. I can't say I mind a flattering review, but there are times when I get pissed that someone has to classify me as mid-Collins, neo-Joplin, Miss Delta Mama, crap like that. Usually it's just a harmless kid trying his best to be significant in a college newspaper so I can even get a kick out of it. If a major publication stooped to that kind of lame excuse for journalism, I'd be pissed, and lose respect for the writer. By and large, all the reviews I've seen have been pretty decent.

How do you feel about criticism?
Do you feel writers have created
an image for you which is incorrect?

At this level of my career, it's like having an infant. When you decide to have a child, you know you're going to have to give up a lot of privacy and free time for a few years until she can take care of herself. Once she's old enough, you can relax and get some of those pieces of yourself back in place. I'm still a "new mother," but it shouldn't be too long before I can take more time off for myself and not run the risk of having all that groundwork disappear. I've tried to base a following on lots of live performances as opposed to hit records, on the assumption that I'll be around a lot longer that way and that somehow this will all fall into place. We'll see.

What about your privacy?
Do you feel like you're
losing your privacy?

I don't do it on purpose. I just find the songs that mean the most to me. They're really not all sad. I'd say they're all basically bluesy tunes in terms of being about men and women and either the problems or good times where that subject is concerned. The Sippie Wallace, delta and dixieland type stuff, as well as the uptempo soul things aren't really what you'd call sad. I think it's probably that the

Is there any reason why
you structure your performances around
such down songs?
It seems as though your songs
are very sad.

slow tunes I do are sad in the extreme, and that's why you might remember them more. I also usually save some of the more painful ones until the end of the set because I'd be a wreck if I did them first. I'm generally pretty happy in between songs, and sometimes it can get very schizzy to have to bounce back and forth between fast and slow tunes, coming out of "Love Has No Pride" and zipping right into a rock and roll tune.

I never said I was holding up. I sing mostly blues songs because they move me. Soul and country music both have the same elements of loneliness, jealousy, "do me right," "I'm leaving," and love as do blues. If that's what's happening, then I sing about it. As for the other things I feel, they don't seem to come out in music, mostly in the wash.

LINDA RONSTADT

Linda Ronstadt has a problem, part of which relates to her own charm and sex appeal, and part of which derives from the rather narrow view male critics have of her. A recent review of her album, *Don't Cry Now*, pronounces: "Looking as she does, an impossibly cuddly chicklet, it's easy to forgive Linda Ronstadt any musical deficiencies. But this album, in fact her first on Asylum, shows off her musical measurements to the best advantage." Thanks a lot.

Linda contributes to the dilemma with her own misplaced sense of insecurity. For complicated reasons, she doesn't simply judge her talent in relation to her audience as much as she compares herself to other performers whom she considers her superiors.

For the record, Linda Ronstadt is one of the finest singers in the medium. She has a clear, strong, vibrant voice, and she is an able interpreter, reading a song with emotion and finesse and her own brand of intuitive insight. She takes her music seriously. On stage she can be excitable, though her performances are ordered and full of energy, and she is backed by consistently fine musicians.

Even though she is just now beginning to study the guitar, Linda has a good ear and has always been demanding of her sidemen. She doesn't lead her band as much as she sings along with it, choosing to assert her feelings during preconcert sound checks, so that when showtime comes, everyone is musically organized.

Linda is at home before rock audiences and has toured the country with the likes of Neil Young and Jackson Browne, playing in such diverse locations as hockey arenas and symphony auditoriums. At the same time, she often plays country and western clubs to rousing audience response. At the Palomino Club in North Hollywood, California, reputed to be the top country and western spot in the West, she has broken all attendance records. Yet Linda is not a country and western singer. Her own musical preferences run strongly to rhythm and blues, the type of music she most frequently chooses to listen to. However, she feels she is "incurably white" as a singer, and perhaps, as she points out, her goal is to show that white music can be soulful too. With this in mind, Linda fuses country and rock into a special union.

Born on July 15, 1946, in Tucson, Arizona, Linda moved to Los Angeles after her freshman semester at the University of Arizona to sing with her friend Bob Kimmel, a singer and guitar player who left Arizona to try to find a career in music. Soon after, they met bass player Kenny Edwards, who shared their musical tastes, and the three of them formed a group they called the Stone Poneys. They recorded three albums and a hit single, "Different Drum," for Capitol Records. All three of the LPs have been cut out of the Capitol catalogue, which means they are no longer available from the distributor. However, owing to Linda's increasing popularity, Capitol recently released an album called *Different Drum*, which is a collection of songs from her older LPs, including some of the early Stone Poneys material.

After the group broke up, Linda recorded three albums on her own for Capitol. These solo efforts included "Hand Sown...Home Grown," "Silk Purse," and "Linda Ronstadt." Her debut album on Asylum, *Don't Cry Now*, was released in September of 1973.

In spite of her continuing success, Linda worries. It seems she has been pidgeonholed to such an extent that she is often given little credit for having any brains. It is somewhat ironic that her appearance should prove a liability. She wears her dark hair straight, bangs framing her face above wide eyes and a bright smile. She is fresh and engaging, traits which seem to accent her often provocative stage manner. Linda likes to feel sexy on stage and the message is communicated as much through her clothes, a wardrobe which includes tight pants and filmy blouses, as through her movements, suggestive comments, and generally friendly attitude. In this way, she sometimes seems to perpetuate her own stereotype.

She has been criticized for allowing the men in her life to make her musical decisions, for being both musically and personally impressionable and an element of surprise is commonplace when she is found to be ingratiating, intelligent, and articulate. Linda Ronstadt is immensely likable, a warm and sensitive person with a genuine will to please. The very fact of her agreeability makes her lack of professional confidence all the more frustrating. She is immensely talented and predictably, purposefully feminine.

The reason Maria is my favorite is that she's the only girl I can think of, who doesn't ever sacrifice an ounce of femininity for what she does. The thing that always hits me about women in rock and roll, myself included, is that there seems to be an incredible amount of competition. If you're really going to be a musician, you have to compete with the boys. You have to be able to talk as dirty and have just as callous an attitude, and it even comes out in your walk eventually.

I can remember when I was a little kid my father used to take my brother hunting all the time, and I wanted to go too because I wanted his attention, to be part of the gang. I was about four. I thought, I have to walk that way and be able to talk that way, and be real tough, and carry my .22, which was bigger than I was. We used to target practice with rotten eggs, and it was important for me to be able to do that. I couldn't do it very well because I was so young, but it meant so much because I was a girl.

My sister was a good shot. She shot a wild pig once, and I thought that was the greatest thing, because she had succeeded in the man's world on a man's terms. To me that was always the ultimate thing you could do. But it's so stupid, and that's the thing that's put on us. But Maria does in fact succeed in a man's world on a man's terms without becoming a man in any way, without becoming masculine in any way. She's always feminine, and it doesn't mean that she has to be receptive and passive and do what she's told, and always come on like a sexpot or anything like that. Her sexuality is so honest and so natural, completely spontaneous and appears so uncalculated and uncontrived. It's refreshing, and I think that's the ideal of being an equal in this world. I mean that's not to say she doesn't get her share

You have mentioned that of all the women in rock and roll, Maria Muldaur is your favorite. Why?

of the things that all women suffer from, the same kind of prejudices, and the same kind of discrimination. She's certainly had to put up with it longer than any of us, but she's still not countered it by becoming butch.

Do you think you've sacrificed any of your femininity?

Oh sure, I've lost a lot of it. I keep trying not to lose it, because I think femininity is real important, even with changing sexual roles. I don't like the idea of women having to look like men. It seems to me they're trying to be something they're not and I don't like it.

Where does that pressure to be one of the boys come from?

Well, it probably comes from myself more than anything. It's just like being a kid again. When I went hunting with my family I wanted to be included and I wanted to be approved of, and I wanted to be a peer. So I tried to do those things well, ride my horse, climb a tree, whatever. Not that I should have been home playing with dolls necessarily. I mean I should have been able to excel at those things, but it should have occurred to me that I should be able to just because I'm a person, not because I was a girl and I was handicapped.

It's the same way when you're out on the road with a bunch of guys. They're your company, they're your family, they're the only people to talk to, and they're the people you look to for approval, for recognition, for having a great time. Eventually, you just start doing what they do. I've always had a foul mouth, even when I was a kid, but when I come off the road now I sound like a truck driver. It's that whole tone of voice, the whole approach, and I hate it.

Also, you get defensive because there's always somebody coming at you with something, so I get down on myself feeling like I'm not really a good enough singer. You get defensive and that makes you act tough and hard. I try to fight against that, too, but you can only fight so long. It gets you eventually, I think. It gets me eventually, all the time.

How directly do you deal with your musicians?

I always have a masculine figure to interpret for me. It's just like having an interpreter for a foreign language. I always try to work through him. I could probably deal directly if I were more of a musician, so I really can't put all the blame on masculine ego's hating to be directed by a female, although that often has much to do with it. I have found that the better the musician, the more sure of himself he is, the less he can ever feel threatened by me and my presence.

It would be a better situation if I were more of a musician myself, but I don't play. When I came out to Los Angeles, I knew a few chords on the guitar, but there were so many men around who played so well that I thought, well, I'm a girl, why should I bother? I'll sing. When you don't play an instrument, your chances for developing musically are so limited. The slower you develop as a musician, and the faster your tastes and your overview develop from hanging around with musicians, then the more you come down on yourself because your taste has in fact developed faster than your ability. So you judge yourself sixteen times as hard. Then you feel farther and farther behind, as though you might as well not even bother trying to catch up. Finally it got to the point last year where I realized it was foolish of me to continue in music if I didn't start to play.

So now I am a beginner guitar player, and I'm finding it a lot easier to communicate my ideas to the band, and the band is a lot more comfortable working with me because they understand me. The result is a better rapport all the way around. It's still incredibly hard, it's never going to be easy. But it's not like it was before, just blind frustration and rage all the time because I couldn't make it right.

I got a piano because I intended to do a particular song on stage and play it, but it just fell by the wayside. I got busy, but it's always like that. It's always, shit, I've got a tour coming up and I've got to rehearse a new band, and I've got to get all the stuff together and I've got a gig coming up, and I'll think about playing the piano next week.

It's that way with health, too. I'll go out on the road and always start out with the best of intentions. For one thing, I run. I really feel that running is my salvation. People have different ways of coping with their situations so they won't be completely driven under by the pressure and the strain of bad food and weird, irregular life-style. My way is running. It absolutely works for me as a depression cure and as a health helper. So I always start out the first week I'm on a tour running every day. I try to eat right. I think, I'm really into it this time. And then there's always a night when I didn't get enough sleep so I don't run, and I'm afraid of eating so I do some cocaine, and I was depressed that night so I take an upper, and then that's the end of it. Then it's uppers and coke for the rest of the tour. And downers to get to bed at night because I can't sleep because I just took an upper. Then I end up getting sick because I'm so allergic to all that stuff. And when uppers start to wear off, you get suicidal.

I'm really sporadic about drugs, like I am about everything else in my life. I'll go for months without anything, it never occurs to me. Occasionally if I go to a party and someone has some coke, I take some. I don't smoke a lot of dope because I'm allergic to it. I really try not to do anything because it's so bad for you, and I know that I'm messing my health up. I keep wondering if it's worth it, because you don't have a long shot at it. Your career is maybe ten or fifteen years, and that isn't much compared to your whole life. Then I get to a gig and I know that I really want to do a good show, I really want to boogie and have a great time and make it good.

When you're performing, energy goes out of you, and it's received by everybody in the audience. If there's 5000 people and you put out one measure of energy, if they like it, they give you 5000 measures back. It multiplies geometrically, and if you don't put it out, and if they don't dig it, it's subtracted from you geometrically. For me that is a real, physical, tangible working item that I have to deal with every single day. If it's drained from you, it can kill you. I think it can make you die, musically just croak, and at the very least, it can make you sick of body and spirit to where you can't move. So there's always that little period before a show when I have to grapple with it.

If things are going badly for me, if I'm on a tour that's long and I'm having a difficult time relating to the audiences, I will always be taking drugs, and if it's relatively easy, it's never easy, but if it's more easy, then I won't be.

I was on tour with Neil Young for a long time, three and half months, and it was incredibly difficult. We were playing 15,000-seat places, coliseums and hockey rinks, and I was playing to Neil's audience. They didn't know I was on the bill because I was added at the last minute after they'd already sold out the whole tour. The anticipation for Neil, who's a cult hero and someone these kids really worship, was just incredible. I really had a tough job going out on stage. The lights would dim and they'd expect to see Neil Young and there I'd be. All the girls in the audience would immediately think, arghh, a girl on tour with Neil, and I'd have to overcome their resentment every single night. I did do really well in the end. That tour was incredibly successful for me. It was responsible I'm sure for "Don't Cry Now" doing as well as it has. But it was a struggle. My confidence was at ground zero. I felt alienated from everybody, and so I took a lot of drugs. I took speed every night, and I'd get up on stage and I thought I was far out. I thought I was great and I was ready to boogie. If you don't think you're great, it communicates immediately to the band and they lose confidence and then they play badly. The tone of the whole set becomes nervous and bad, but if I go up there thinking I'm hot, they think they're hot, too, and so we do a good show. You always have that choice to make. It's awful.

I've never been happy with myself as a singer. I never thought I was very good. I never wanted to be a single to begin with. When I was a kid, I always sang with my sister and brother. It was always an ensemble situation and I always sang harmonies. So I think I'm a better harmony singer than I am a lead singer. I love to watch Clydie King and Merry Clayton and Shirley Matthews sing backup. Those girls to me are real musicians. They're just like the lead guitar player or the bass player or the drummer. They stand up on stage and just riff away. Maybe the thing that makes a lead singer and a person who can be considered a star, is always something that has to do more with being unique, and being able to say it for people in a way that no one else can. But it doesn't necessarily mean that you're really a good musician. I'm always comparing myself to other people. I try to be as creative as I can, but it's just a battle you have to fight all the time.

Someone once said that competition is for horse races and not for art. It's true because it's really life-destroying and it destroys creative processes when you start to compete. For me it does anyway, because there's always going to be somebody better.

Do you think you are a different person on stage than you are off stage?

No, I'm not different, I'm just edited. It's funny. Sometimes I'm really at my worst up there. Maybe I'm more the same than I even think I am.

When I meet somebody new, I'm kind of at their mercy. What they think of me will almost invariably be the attitude that I assume. In other words, if I meet somebody with whom I think I have no credibility, somebody who things I'm a lightweight, whether they do or not, that's the way I end of up being to them. And I have to fight with that with audiences every night.

Being on stage is like being at a cocktail party with a bunch of people that you don't know and nobody gets to talk but you. You have to carry on the entire conversation. An audience can project a lot on me, more than I'm sure they realize, so I'm always dealing with some form of insecurity or other. I compensate for it accordingly, sometimes by just standing up there and not saying anything at all and just singing, and sometimes by really trying to charm them. I do the same things on an individual level.

Do you try to be sexy on stage?

Yes, I always do. That's rough too, because when I first started doing it, I thought that was what you were supposed to do. I really felt that if I was sexy enough, they'd like me no matter what. I always used that to try to compensate for everything, to make people like me. I did that all my life as a kid, too. And it was always a problem, because if you come on sexy like that, that's the response you get, you get a sexy reaction. However, it's not necessarily flattering, it's not necessarily intelligent, and it doesn't necessarily have anything to do with the music. Very often, it's detrimental to the way people think of you.

I've always had the problem of people thinking I'm a piece of cheese, so then the next time I go out on stage I think, oh they already have this preconceived notion of me, and they think I can't think or talk, and then it will keep pinning me into that situation. But a lot of women will fall back on that when they feel insecure. It gets horrifying when you think that your looks are going to run out, or your charm. It's unfair.

Dr. John, for instance is someone I adore. He dispenses so much joy and comfort. He's like Santa Claus, he's like a good demon, the demon of joy. He comes out on stage and throws gris-gris around and sings so great. He turns around and gives you that great toothless grin he's got and he's so huge. Whenever I see him I think, here's a person who breaks all the rules of good looks. He's got a tooth missing, he's enormously fat and wears all these weird clothes. He doesn't have perfect skin, and he doesn't look like those people on television in the ads. But to me, he's incredibly sexy, and the audience loves him.

If a chick did that, forget it. The chicks that are up on stage with him look really good. A girl can't really get away with that. A girl can't have unusual features to set the standards for what's beautiful and what's sexy and what's great and what isn't. I'm sure there are exceptions, but they are very few.

For me, when I meet a guy and fall in love with him, his looks automatically become that standard of what I think is great. For guys, I think it's more the Playboy model standard and I think it's so unfair. It makes me furious that women are subjected to this guideline of what they're supposed to look like, instead of becoming their own guidelines.

I've gone sort of back and forth between going on stage trying to look as glamorous as possible, and going on stage trying to just look regular. I did a year when I just wore street clothes all the time because I thought, well shit, no one's ever going to take me seriously if I go on stage in shorts and spangles and looking like a piece of cheese. But on the other hand, I really think that's part of it, too. I think that's part of the comfort.

Audiences like to see somebody winning, they like to see somebody who's overcome that kind of everyday gray. That's why I love to see Dr. John in all his feathers. And the Pointer Sisters standing up on stage looking so fine. That really helps me. So I started dressing up again. I just don't know. You just have to get up there and do the best you can and hope it's right.

Being an entertainer, especially in times like these, is really a public service. But it's really hard. There was a long time when I felt I was being imposed on because I had to go out on stage and sing. It was a bad attitude to have. Now I see that I am really there to perform a service for people and I think it would be immoral for me to take their money and not give them relief.

Sometimes they are because they always act their worst around you. People have some preconceived notion of you. They feel they know you because they have heard you express your intimate feelings. My songs are always expressions of exactly what's going on in my life. Even though I didn't write them, I try to interpret myself through them. So people think that you should know them, too. Then when they see you and they realize that you don't know them at all, it makes them defensive and lots of times they become ugly, and there's hardly any way to protect yourself from it.

Are fans a hassle?

I see that in concerts, too, especially in those great big halls, like I played with Neil. In a crowd that big you lose your identity, and not only are you anonymous, but there's one person on stage who as all the attention, all the identification. People get defensive because the contrast is so enormous between identity and anonymity. Kids get crazy in those situations, and that's when they start yelling out "Boogie," or they throw frisbees. They want to make an impression, they want to do something that registers. It's terrifying to deal with because people can get so ugly.

I don't ever like to stand alone before a concert so that people can come up and talk to me. They say the lamest things. They try to be nice. They want to say that they like the music or something, but they end up saying things that intentionally or unintentionally become horribly insulting. It's as if they're embarrassed about the fact that they're fans, so they try to be cool, and they cop an attitude of nonchalance. It's so often insulting that you just end up feeling like you never want to see another human being. It makes you so defensive you eventually have to go underground if you're sensitive. It gets harder and harder to surface each time.

It's funny how it affects relationships, too. For me to have a relationship with a man is so preposterous. First of all, men are threatened by what I do, just as I am threatened by what they do. But they're threatened on a lot of different levels. If they're in the business and they're not as well known as I am, or if they're in the business and they don't think they're as good as I am, they feel threatened. Then if they're in the business and they're a lot better than I am, I'm threatened by comparing myself.

I lived with a guy for two and a half years who was a good singer and songwriter and a much better musician than I am. I had that every day to compare myself to. It ended up that I'd get up every morning and fix breakfast and he'd write a song. He'd be playing the guitar while I'd be in cooking eggs, and I used to get pissed off. I used to think that I should be playing the guitar, but I wouldn't because he'd be there and he was better than I was and I'd figure what's the use.

So there's all those aspects of it, plus there's the fact that I'm an attractive person who has to deal with a lot of other attractive people. The people in show business all have some kind of personal magnetism or they wouldn't be able to get on stage. All that magnetism works on each other all the time, and so relationships become so incestuous after a while. The sex pool is like the musicians' pool in this town. Get one out, have him for a while, throw him back in. There's a threat, knowing that people are always going to be attracted, so you're never really safe. If you're married to a shoe salesman for instance, the kind of people he's going to meet in his business are limited, so the chances of having a monogamous relationship are automatically increased.

Then there's the problem of traveling all the time. Relationships are always interrupted. The temptation is to deal in a relationship just on a surface level and to only go so deep, because as soon as it comes to a point where you encounter some real resistance from another person, encounter a problem that takes some real working out, some mature attitudes, which I'm going to develop maybe next week, you can always leave town. It's a pop attitude.

It's the same with a song on the radio. It's popular for three months and then you get tired of it, so you find another one. It's the same with clothing styles. I think we've all been geared by the economy somehow to change over every three years or every three months or every six months, depending on which commodity it is that you're dealing with. In the case of automobiles, it's every two years, in the case of relationships, it seems to me to be every year, if that. A heavy relationship for me lasts a year. The longest relationship I've ever had lasted two and a half years, and it begins to feel pretty pointless after a while. Pretty soon you can't relate to anybody on any level whatsoever.

I'm still pretty close with my family, but what I do is so different from anything in their world. It's funny, but the person I relate to best in my family is my brother who's a cop. The reason is that he has to deal with the public every day, an enormous cross section of people. He has to cope with incredible paranoia because of his job, and I do too.

Are most of your friends in the music business?

It seems to work out that way, although my roommate isn't. It works out that way because of our life-styles. I don't know anybody else who keeps the same hours I do. That becomes a further crippling force in my life, too, because it makes me narrower. Pretty soon I can't talk about anything except what kind of a mix somebody got on his record or how they e.q.'d the bass on that record. You try, but you have nothing to talk about. Also, musician's slang doesn't communicate that well.

I went to Mexico after the Neil Young tour to be completely removed from the music business. I met an anthropologist from Sweden who'd only read English and hadn't spoken it very much. He actually spoke it just about better than I did, but I couldn't communicate with him because my slang was so heavy. I kept having to explain myself and finally I just gave up. I was so disappointed because I fancied having a great romance. It was rough trying to deal with it.

Yes, people do. Always ones I'm not interested in. The neat ones never do because they're too cool, they have too much class. It's a problem because I have no self-control. When I meet somebody I really admire and I trust, which has to be with somebody I'm involved with businesswise, I always end up having a sexual relationship with him. Then it blows it, because as soon as the sexual relationship intrudes, the defense comes up, clang. It's like an iron gate, I'm so defensive, and most of the people I work with are defensive. It always gets in the way.

Fortunately, I have a manager now I'm not having a relationship with. But the last manager, I did. It's weird. He started out to be my boyfriend, then he was managing me and was my producer. Then he wasn't my boyfriend, but he was still managing me and producing me. Then he wasn't producing me but he was still managing me, and then he wasn't managing me any more. All those troubles stem from the fact that in our personal relationship, we couldn't resolve things.

*Is it rough
working around men all the time?
Do they come on to you?*

I grew up in Tucson, and one of the major influences on my life was Mexican music. My father sang it, and sang it great. I grew up listening to mariachi music, which I still love, and which believe it or not, had a strong influence on my singing style.

My sister, who was a complete country music freak, fell in love with Hank Williams when I was six. She used to moon over his picture and she had all his records and played them twenty-four hours a day. She used to listen to the radio, station XERF which came from Del Rio, Texas, but had a transmitter in Acuña, Mexico. It had an incredibly strong signal, and in the daytime they would play Top 40 and country music, and then in the evening it would progress on to rhythm and blues.

Late at night on XERF you could hear what we called "race records" in those days, which was strong R&B stuff, records you wouldn't hear any place around Arizona, because there were no people like that singing that kind of music. On Sundays, they played half white gospel and half black gospel. You'd get an incredible musical amalgamation listening to that radio station. I have to give it credit for a strong influence on my musical background.

My sister and two brothers were musical and we all sang together.

*Would you say something
about your background, about
growing up in Arizona?
About your musical influences?*

I sang all the time when I was growing up. We used to sing with my father, too. He really gave me a keen appreciation for every kind of music. I was always trying to shut myself off musically, depending on what I thought was hip at the time, and he was always fighting me, always saying that there's great music in everything. He turned me on to singers like Billie Holiday and Peggy Lee and Ella Fitzgerald. A teenager growing up in Tucson who is listening to Top 40 radio is not going to be exposed to those singers or think that they are in any way hip, and they're fantastic. I really have my father to thank for a lot of that, even though at the time, I fought him every inch of the way.

My father was a singer during the Depression, but the times were so hard he ended up working in my grandfather's business. My grandfather owned a ranch and my father worked as a cowboy and now my father has taken over his hardware business in Tucson.

By the time I came along, my father was a businessman, but I grew up in the country. He still had an appreciation for the outdoors, a real sensitivity for the desert and for wild animals. He taught me how to shoot and ride and how to love the outdoors. We had horses and lots of animals and he made us fond of all of it.

I hated school. I went to Catholic school and it just warped me completely because I had a really free existence when I was a kid. It was lonely because we lived so far away from town, but it was free. I had a pony and I was like a kid with a car. I could go any place I wanted. I used to ride five or ten miles a day, go off into the mountains all by myself if I wanted.

Then I went to school and it was so structured. The nuns were uptight and I thought they were prudes. I hated them. I wanted to shock them all the time. I used to swear all the time, and I was boy crazy and they hated that. That was where the whole sexy thing started. I wanted to be sexy, I wanted to kiss boys, I wanted them to like me, to pay attention to me. I was always very competitive for masculine attention, I got so much disapproval from the nuns and fought it so hard, I became very rebellious. The sexy thing became my method of rebellion and it's still with me. I still fight the world with that. It's really crippling sometimes.

When did the thought occur to you to try to make a career in music?

When I was about six. As I said, I hated school. I couldn't add, I still can't add. I could read because my mother had taught me to read. I still read voraciously. But I can't figure out a tip on a bill, I can't make change. I thought, well this is never going to make it so I'm going to sing. I daydreamed all the way through school and it was mostly about being a singer, or being in love.

I started singing in clubs around Tucson with my brother and sister when I was in high school. I went to one semester of college and during my Easter vacation I came to Los Angeles to spend a week with Bobby Kimmel, and we sang at some folk club.

It never occurred to me that I was singing in some folk music dive that had fans of some music that had already gone under water. It never occurred to me that they liked me for any reason other than that I was good enough to make it. I mean I wasn't good enough. I wasn't a good singer, and I didn't know what I was doing. I had some instinctive ability which must have communicated itself to the audience, but I think it was mostly my enthusiasm which they felt. We met Kenny Edwards and got together as the Stone Poneys and did three albums for Capitol. I'm not too proud of the stuff I did then, but everybody has to learn.

How do you feel about the music business and the whole music scene?

The thing that bothers me most about the music scene is the intense pressure that people feel on them to be cool. That's bullshit. It doesn't help your music any, and it doesn't help yourself out as a person. Everybody's so careful, they're always checking themselves out, making sure they're not doing something that's uncool.

There are various cliques that have varying degrees of pressure to be cool. The Asylum clique has got it, whew! it's really got it. It's great too, because those people are really out there boogying. But on the other hand, there's a tremendous amount of competition that goes down among all of us, and I don't like to have any part of it. I like to think of myself as divorced from it but I'm sure I'm not.

Do you think that rock and roll is a lonely business?

It's incredibly lonely. Everybody I know is lonely. It has to be that way because of the life-style, all the traveling, the paranoia, the fact that your ass is on the line when you go on stage. It's on the line every single night. I never get over stage fright. I never know how it's going to be. Even when I'm on stage, I never know whether it's going to turn sour or not when I'm right in the middle of doing it. So I'm always on edge. There's always that pressure that I might fall over the edge. That just has to affect relationships.

Rock and roll is a lot warmer than the movie business. I have been able to make really close friends with other women in music. Most of the actresses I know are not able to do that with other actresses. The competition is on such an absurd level for looks and charm and glamour.

The glamour part of rock and roll irritates me, too. In a way, I'm all for glamour because it's an escape. It can take your mind off the mundane and the painful things of life, but on the other hand, it's blown way out of proportion. It has become an idol and it doesn't deserve that position. But glamour makes you feel like you have an identity, and you're totally safe from everything, you're privileged.

If you're beautiful, you're even more privileged, but in a way you're debilitated if you're beautiful. I've never been beautiful. I've never felt like a beauty because I don't have good skin, I don't have good hair, I don't have good features. But I have felt glamorous. I feel like I project an illusion of glamour. But then when you do that, you end up competing with yourself.

If I meet a guy and he's seen my album cover pictures and thinks I'm real pretty, or seen me on television at my best with eight tons of makeup to make my nose look straight and thin and make it look like I have cheekbones and long eyelashes, and then he sees me in person and sees that I really have a terrible case of acne and my hair is always a mess, and I have a terrible problem trying to keep my weight down, I'm afraid he's going to be disappointed and be turned off by it, and so that makes me nervous when people come close. I get crazy. So you end up competing with yourself and the competition is bad enough with other people in the world. When you have to compete with yourself, it's a nightmare.

Sometimes I think my mission is to do country-rock. I really want people to know what the roots are in country music. I want white people to realize that their music is soulful, too. Even though I mostly listen to black music, I'm incurably white as a singer. I want people to be conscious of white soul and what it is.

Do you have any specific career goals?

When I just learn a new song, when it's a great song and I know I can sing it well, that makes me happier than anything in the world except for falling in love. Those two things will do it. I stop eating, I don't get paranoid, I feel like I can look people right in the eye and become their friend and relate to them well, and I don't feel like I have to apologize for myself all the time. When that happens, I'm really happy for a long time. At least a week.

What do you like most about your work?

No, I'm basically an unhappy person. I used to think that people were either basically happy or basically unhappy, and that it didn't change. Now I'm not so sure. Some people do change, but it's so very hard.

Do you think you are basically a happy person?

Yes, it has helped an awful lot. It has helped me realize where a lot of frustrations come from. Before, I was just sort of bogged down by them and I couldn't quite figure out what I was supposed to be. Here

Has the woman's movement made you more conscious of yourself as a woman?

I was, a chick who traveled around and had an enormous amount of independence. I didn't relate to men like other women did, and men didn't relate to me like they did to other women. Being more aware of things has helped me deal with it.

I think the women's movement is important. I think it's vital. I think it's important for men, too. If women can stop having to be dependent on men, then men won't have to be so threatened. I think the women's movement should make women less of a threat to men, not more of a threat. I think it should reduce the tension between the sexes.

What positive contribution to your life do you think rock and roll has made?

Rock and roll has given me an enormous overview, one that I never would have gained if I'd dropped out of school when I did and had stayed in Tucson and become a housewife. It's given me a way to force feed information into my head. Educationally, it's been an enormous plus factor, because I've always wanted to learn.

Sometimes I see my life as a race between me and a kind of hound that's always nipping at my heels. It's a kind of black dog that's suicidal and existential and thinks that life is meaningless and that we're down here and it's an incredible joke at our expense. We're here in this universe, on this planet, spinning around in the cosmos somewhere, and it's just nonsense and it doesn't mean anything.

Then somehow learning new things distracts me from those feelings. Information is my comfort, it's like a drug in a way for me. I can't turn to religion, and I'm too allergic to drugs. So I have that. It's saved me. I don't know what's going to happen when I get to the point where I can't deal with it anymore.

Music is my salvation but it's also my downfall. It's the destruction of everything in me that's sane and good. But I'm glad I've done it. I like the people I've met, I've made some real close friends. It's given me the ability to read people and because of that I can kind of protect myself from them. It's strengthened my instincts. I function on more of an instinctive level now, more than on an intellectual level.

Also, traveling to so many different parts of the country has helped me see the environments which shape people. I understand people better, why they are the way they are. I think I'm more tolerant, a lot more broadminded. But, still, it narrows you down so much. It makes you have to defend yourself so much and protect yourself so much that there you are, kind of locked away with all this amazing amount of insight and information that you acquire from traveling all the time, but not able to put them into practice as well as you would be if maybe you were a little bit more normal and had regular relationships.

CARLY SIMON

Carly Simon grew up in Riverdale, New York, a member of the Simon & Schuster publishing clan, surrounded by wealth and the people that money and literary connections attract. Her career in music began in the folk years of the 1960s, when she sang in a duo with her sister. Billed as the Simon Sisters, they fell short of national fame, but Carly was determined to make a go of music as a career.

Tall and stately, with full features and light brown hair, Carly Simon's musical asset is her voice. While she plays piano and guitar, it is her singing that has proved to be her greatest asset—that, and the kinds of songs she sings, many of which she has written.

In 1971, she signed with Elektra Records and has since recorded four albums, *Carly Simon*, *Anticipation*, *No Secrets*, and, most recently, *Hotcakes*. Moderate radio play and national tours helped attract a growing following that was greatly amplified in 1973 by her first hit single, "You're So Vain," written by Carly and included in her third LP. The song was cleverly promoted in the rock press with a kind of teaser campaign designed to generate speculation as to the subject of the song's sarcastic put-down. Mick Jagger sang backup vocals, a fact that was also highly publicized and that was noticeably audible on the record. It was finally determined that "You're So Vain" was vaguely about Warren Beatty, but, by that time, the song was a national smash nonetheless. When her next album, *Hotcakes*, was released in early 1974, it was a certified gold record ($1 million in sales) the first week it was out.

In November 1972, Carly married singer-songwriter James Taylor, and their first child, Sarah Maria, was born in January 1974.

This chapter, as it turned out, was the most frustrating one in the book for me. Early in 1973, a publicity representative of Elektra called to find out whether I might be interested in doing a piece on Carly for the Sunday Los Angeles *Times*. The *Times* accepted the idea, but was booked solid in the rock and roll department and asked me not to rush the copy. Since Carly, who lives in New York, was planning to be in Los Angeles during the summer, we made tentative plans to meet. Nothing ever came of it.

In November I called Carly's manager in New York, Arlyne Rothberg, and asked if Carly would give me an interview for this book. Then began a seemingly endless series of phone calls. First, the interview, which was to be done by phone, had to wait because Carly was rushing to finish *Hotcakes*; then it was postponed because Carly was expecting her baby "any day"; then I was told she couldn't do anything until two weeks after her baby was born.

Toward the beginning of February, already behind deadline, I was still getting the runaround. Finally, in mid-february I made what I was determined was to be one last phone call to Arlyne Rothberg, and told her secretary, "now or never." Half an hour later Carly returned my call. She was pleasant and cheerful, but distracted by her baby, who was suffering from a bad cold. We decided that talking on the phone wouldn't work, but Carly offered to send a written reply to any questions I might have.

I had quite a few. Aside from the usual questions about background, incentives, pitfalls, and problems, I wanted to know specific things about Carly's music. She writes many of her own songs, some in collaboration with writer Jacob Brackman and others with her musicians. There are disturbing themes that recur consistently: a preoccupation with childhood, sibling rivalry, family acceptance, the conflict between the romantic myths of relationships and the seemingly insecure realities. These were rather unusual concerns for someone who will reach thirty this year and I was interested to find out whether she recognizes this element of reiteration of material and how she feels about it.

I sent Carly my list of questions and shortly thereafter received a reply, the contents of which follow. At the beginning she remarked, "There seem to be a lot of questions! First of all, I would love to be able to give them a whole lot of thought and come up with responses for all of them; but time is of the essence and Sarah is a demanding and relatively sleepless infant. So, I shall try to answer the questions I feel most comfortable with as thoroughly as I can."

Here is Carly's reply, which I am happy to include, but disappointed in because of its brevity. Carly Simon is one of the best known of all women in popular music and her feelings and thoughts are important in that context. Hopefully, there will be other opportunities to explore those feelings in the future.

I becomes easier and easier to express my own musical ideas in the studio. It's always hard to translate into words what can only be expressed musically, therefore to have as many musicians as I can to whom I have to say as little as possible is very important. I have worked with Richard Perry as a producer for my two most recent albums, and by now there is a nice understanding between us. When you work day in and day out with the same person, you develop your own language, that is, if it's a successful relationship.

I have had experiences where I have had to use more and more words and they were understood less and less. Although Richard has been referred to as a Svengali, and he certainly has those qualities, I have a great deal to say about what goes down in the studio. I work with Richard, and not for him. We are both strong and argue (though it is often more like banter) over both fundamental musical concepts and specific notes and chords.

No, my producer doesn't make most of the decisions. If it comes down to the wire, Richard always bows rather gracefully and lets me have my way, although later I occasionally regret it.

I have a lot of respect for Richard, he is the most energetic and undauntable man I know, and he has the rather rare, but spectacular ability to perfect a complicated e.q. (adding lows, highs, etc.) while carrying on two telephone conversations and ordering Thai noodles from Teperod Thai as *well* as consoling and assuring me that he is totally "on the case." He also has a wonderful sense of humor and likes to laugh and waste time as much as I do. Hence, I love to make records. There's a special atmosphere about each one. It's like individual summers at camp. The end of an album is gloriously sad.

I feel relaxed in a recording studio. If you record an entire album in one studio, you begin to leave things there, like a sweater or a special mug for your own tea. Then, artistically I like it because it mixes spontaneity with a kind of deliberateness. Something like controlled chaos.

Usually when I go into a session, I haven't rehearsed the tune beforehand and barely have a lead sheet. This does not make monetary good sense, but it allows every person involved to make a personal statement. The element of chance...Certainly a live performance (stage, club) offers that, but somehow I fear not being able to rescind the limb I have gone out on. But that's just my particular Achilles' heel.

I feel too vulnerable out on stage—as if everything depends upon it. Otherwise, I like being on the road. I like eating junk food and breaking the seal on Holiday Inn toilets. Not for too long, but while I was doing it, I liked the road aspects of it.

As performance time drew nigh, I grew more and more weary and homesick. But when I'm on the road with James I really enjoy myself. I like to feel part of his show but removed enough to avoid the stage fright. I'm great at calling room service and warding off untimely visitors. (This is not a sexist answer. I'd feel the same if I were on the road with my aunt.)

James has a great many fans of both sexes and I have noticed that his female fans don't make any bones about just wanting to meet him or touch him, whereas his male fans are less comfortable in their fanmanship and introduce themselves as protégés. Girls are much more tactile as fans, more unabashed about hero worship.

I don't know whether being married discourages our fans of the opposite sex. I think it may encourage girls who want to be like me when they grow up, 'cause marriage is such a part of a little girl's upbringing—something to attain. Maybe it doesn't even enter into it. I used to worship Odetta and I didn't even know if she was married.

Criticism affects every performer no matter what they say or how many times they promise not to read their reviews. The good ones make me feel good and the bad ones, lousy, which is at least a step above not believing the good ones and thinking they've really got your number every time anything negative about you is uttered. Sometimes I can rationalize the bad ones and say he or she doesn't like me because he or she is a frustrated singer and is jealous that I have had a certain amount of success. Or, more logically, that not everyone has the same taste.

It has surprised me upon occasion that a performer I had thought was so together in areas of self-respect, has been rendered disconsolate by a bad review.

I have a hard time accepting success. I feel guilty about it. It's as if, if I'm successful, someone else has to suffer for it. I think it's based on sibling rivalry and the unfounded notion that if your parents love one child they can't love the other as well. If you're the one who is getting the love at that time and place you feel superior, as if you're eating two-thirds of the pie. The point is, there is, or should be, room for everyone to be loved and no one to feel guilty about getting too much. It all sounds very cliché-ish. Guilt gets to be boring after a while.

James and I deal with our feelings of competition with each other all the time. They are difficult to express to each other, often because we feel ashamed about having such "base emotions."

Sometimes I decide in a fit of guilt that I will take backseat to James and take up the traditional role of "the woman standing behind the man." We'd both hate me for it though. I want to feel more like a unit—so that what's his success is mine and vice versa.

Were so conscious of the problem now that it's much easier to deal with and we admit and often laugh about jealousy. It's such an animal emotion. Especially in the area of possessiveness. Dogs growl. I growl too, but very, very quietly and I've learned to make it almost inaudible by shrouding it in pleasantries.

Our personal life is hardly limited by our being in the music business unless you consider being asked for an autograph a serious infringement on privacy. I don't mind it and my only complaint is people who come by our house without our knowing them, or people that we hardly know asking for favors because in their minds we have everything and they have nothing.

The baby is another matter entirely. She's five weeks old and there's no such thing as privacy now. She's watching everything we do. The question is, is she an extension of James and me? Does our privacy encompass her or exclude her? Right now she is crying for food or attention or to be changed or some amorphous baby blues and I must conclude this rambling essay. The baby I'm sure will affect my career. It's got to make me think differently as a writer in that all kinds of consciousnesses are different. I'll grow to know myself better. Having a baby, I seek to define myself in different ways. I want to know who it is that has had her. What, in her, do I recognize in myself, her mom? She sure has temper tantrums!

I realize I haven't talked much about how it is to be "a woman" as opposed to "a man" in show biz. It's partly because I don't feel that line of demarcation as strongly as some other women do and it's not a central issue at the moment, although I do wish James would change Sarah's diapers more often!

GRACE SLICK

Grace Wing Slick is not someone to be taken lightly. She is perhaps one of the most well-known of all rock and roll women, and as one of the lead singers for Jefferson Airplane, has been in the public eye since the early 1960s.

Her visual trademarks have been her long, curly, dark hair and model good looks. She is slender, sophisticated, and yet has chosen to follow highly contemporary styles. Her most stunning attribute, however, is her voice, (clear and hearty,) which seems to somehow flow around her music, turning at times into a throaty vibrato that is impressive in its strength.

Grace has also contributed numerous songs to the Airplane's repertoire. As she points out, one of her most prominent characteristics is sarcasm, which is frequently expressed in her compositions. In "Eskimo Blue Day" she challenges, "You call it rain/But the human name/Doesn't mean shit to a tree."

The sarcasm is coupled with an icy veneer she often exhibits to complement her often uninhibited behavior. From the beginning of her identification with rock and roll, Grace has displayed an almost contrived weirdness, as if she were going out of her way to be strange. She has pursued the unconventional, defying the social norm and challenging the existing order. There has been an almost constant emphasis on drugs. These elements have simultaneously attracted and repelled audiences. Her blatant aggressiveness has proved to be both an asset and a liability. In some ways, Grace Slick has become the alter ego, the fantasy representation of a contradictory freedom which most women do not, or dare not, pursue on a realistic level.

There are volumes of Grace Slick escapades. One of the most repeated is about a shopping trip she made to an Aston-Martin auto dealer in San Francisco. Dressed as she was, rather unconventionally in what came to be know as "hippie sleek," Grace walked around the showroom admiring the cars. She was duly ignored. Finally, when a salesman did approach her, she pointed at a particularly expensive model and said, "I'll have that one." And proceeded to pay cash.

Such stories have been passed around for years, exaggerated and modified. Their truth is not as important as the fact that Grace has been a more or less constant topic of conversation among a tightly knit number of rock and roll fanatics. The anecdotes point out that Grace is independent and fierce about her priorities.

Among the most important items in her life now are her daughter China, whose father is Airplane guitarist Paul Kantner with whom she has been living for the past few years, her music, and Tae Kwon Do karate, the Korean form of the martial art which is reputed to be particularly violent.

Grace grew up in San Francisco and loved music and art and the movies. She was semiseriously considering a career in some facet of filmmaking when she became attracted to popular music, specifically the growing rock and roll community in the city in which she was living.

She and her former husband, Jerry Slick, visited the Matrix, a small club that was featuring a new rock group, Jefferson Airplane. Intrigued by the music and by the fact that it looked like fun, Grace and Jerry put together their own group, the Great Society. When the Great Society dissolved shortly thereafter, and the Airplane's female singer took a maternity leave, Grace joined Paul Kantner, Jorma Kaukonen, Jack Casady, Marty Balin, and Spencer Dryden, and the Airplane became San Francisco's bellwether group.

Jefferson Airplane played what was referred to at the time as "psychedelic" or "acid" rock, which was a combination of folk influences and early rock and roll heavily laced with a large number of drug references. Their performances usually included light shows, and mood was as important as music.

Grace brought with her a good deal of material from the Great Society, including "Somebody To Love" and her own classic "White Rabbit." The Airplane appeared at the 1967 Monterey Pop Festival, Woodstock, and the Altamont, California, gathering that was the subject of the Rolling Stones' film, *Gimme Shelter*, finding themselves in the center of many massive pop culture happenings.

Between 1967 and 1971, Grace and the Airplane released six albums on RCA Records, including *Surrealistic Pillow*, *After Bathing at Baxter's*, *Crown of Creation*, *Bless Its Pointed Little Head*, *Volunteers*, and *The Worst of Jefferson Airplane*, a collection of songs from the previous LPs. Grace also appeared on Paul Kantner's solo album, *Blows Against The Empire*, which was the last album they did for the label.

In mid-1971, the Airplane formed its own company, Grunt Records, and the group continued to diversify. Jorma Kaukonen and Jack Casady pursued their interest in the blues with Hot Tuna, and Grace and Paul again recorded together. The Airplane's Grunt LPs include *Bark, Long John Silver,* and *Thirty Seconds Over Winterland.* Grace and Paul collaborated on *Sunfighter,* and added David Freiberg on *Baron Von Tollbooth and The Chrome Nun.*

Capitalizing on Grace's success with Jefferson Airplane, Columbia Records released three albums in 1970 and 1971, of old Great Society material.

In late January 1974, Grace's first solo LP, *Manhole* was released. It was her first venture into singing with an orchestra, and, in part, offers the Spansih musical influences she likes so much. *Manhole* is a musical experiment for Grace, but a logical extension of the growing independence of the individual Airplane members.

The Grunt ad for the album calls Grace "The voice that launched a thousand trips." For a while, when people were talking about San Francisco as some sort of popular culture mecca, when there were so-called "flower children" and "be-ins" and music cascaded out of the Fillmore and Winterland ballrooms, there seemed to be only two recognized rock and roll ladies. One was Grace Slick. The other was her friend, Janis Joplin.

*When did you decide
that you wanted to sing professionally?*

I never really thought of it as a career. There was a picture of Marty Balin in the newspaper, and he looked like a cross between Oriental, and maybe a little Black and a little Spanish or something. It was an appealing picture because I'd never seen an Oriental rock and roll singer. It turned out he's not, it was just the way the picture looked. So Jerry Slick and I went down to see who this far-out looking guy was, he looked so weird in the paper.

It looked like he was having fun. He was with Jefferson Airplane and they were just starting out. We thought, hell, we can do that, they're just dirty hippies like we are. So we started a group called the Great Society. Then a couple of guys from the Great Society decided that they liked Indian music, so they were going to go off to India and do that. And Signe Anderson, the girl singer for the Airplane, was pregnant at the time and she was going to go off and have her baby. I didn't really do it for a career, it just looked like it would be fun to do.

*Had you thought
about doing anything else?*

Oh sure, movies. I wanted to do anything I could get, soundtracks, acting, production, animation, photography. I like movies a lot. It wasn't my absolute preference as to what to do, because I like to draw, and I like to paint, and there's a whole bunch of stuff which is interesting to me. It didn't really make a difference what I did, since there were, and are, so many things which I like and any of them would be all right.

Grace Slick / 153

Were you ever concerned with the fact that you are a woman in front of an all-male band?

No, not really. Peggy Lee is a woman in front of an all-male band. There was nothing very unusual about that. Lena Horne, Barbra Streisand sing with an all-male band. There aren't too many women who play saxophone. It wasn't particularly difficult on the road, either. The only thing that would have been hard was to have to change clothes. There were always people around, everybody would have all their friends around in the dressing room. But it wasn't a problem. I always got dressed in my hotel room.

In general, people were very pleasant to me. Very normal. There's a lot of talk about women's lib and all this junk, but I never thought about it. If I acted like an asshole, I was treated like an asshole. If I acted regular, I was treated regular. It didn't seem more difficult because I was a woman.

Was there ever any problem about having your feelings taken into consideration, about songs you wanted to record, about arrangements?

At the time, Paul would write three or four songs, I would write three or four, or we'd do some Great Society stuff, or Jorma would write some. Everybody more or less had a number of songs. Now Jorma and Jack formed Hot Tuna because they like blues and also because they prefer instrumentals to vocalizing. The Airplane is sort of a massive rush of vocals. Sometimes it seems like we're all up there yelling. So Jack and Jorma formed Hot Tuna so they could do the instrumental material they like so well.

Did you ever feel as though you wanted to play an instrument with the group?

No, I don't think they would have liked that at all. We had plenty of instruments. Paul plays twelve-string guitar, Jorma's guitar is pretty loud, and Jack's bass is loud. I don't think we needed any more than we had.

However, I do play piano and I think that now I might try to play on stage. I don't know whether I'll like it or not, but I'll find out. I may hate it. I prefer standing up to sing, though, because with rock and roll it's hard to get those notes out sitting down. You're all kind of hunched up. If you sing soft songs, you can sing sitting down, but it's tough to sing rock and roll sitting down. I might play the piano parts on the records and let someone else play them on stage while I'm singing. I'm not really sure whether I'll play piano on stage or not. I may play if somebody else wants to sing.

Do you think things would have been different for you if you had begun as a solo act, rather than being with a group?

I think it would have bored a lot of people. It wouldn't have been harder, I think it would have been boring. An hour and a half of the same thing. I can't think of too many people I want to see for an hour and a half all by themselves. I like to see a variety in the show.

I do my sarcastic songs and Paul does his happy, let's-get-together songs, and Jorma does his blues. I thought it was interesting that way. We had a lot of people writing and a lot of different styles. A solid hour and a half of my sarcasm would be very boring.

I'm more or less the same off stage. I'm just as obnoxious off stage. Stage actors, theatre people, will get off the stage and all of a sudden they're very quiet just after they've played Henry VIII. But I've noticed that film people seem to be another story. Steve McQueen is always Steve McQueen. I think rock and roll people are more or less like that. I met Mick Jagger and he's not quite that jive, so he's more of a stage performer. But most of the people I know are very much like they are on stage, off stage.

*Do you feel as though
you are the same person off stage
as you are on stage?*

Oh sure, that's always fun to do now and then. I like to look sexy. Sometimes I like to look peculiar, too. I dressed like Hitler once. It's fun to put on costumes and act like a jerk. I enjoy it. Sometimes it's sexy, sometimes it's funny, sometimes it's evil. It's just a matter of being hammy. It doesn't depend on my mood too much, because you have to plan ahead. If you're in New York, you have to have brought a certain amount of stuff with you. So obviously, I knew I was going to do Hitler one night. The particular night is sort of up to your mood. As a matter of fact, I think Hitler was impromptu. Mostly it has to be planned if you're going to be on the road, because you have to take whatever you are going to do with you. You can't all of a sudden drag something out of your closet, because your closet isn't there.

Do you try to be sexy on stage?

Through letters, yes. I don't see that many people who are fans because I take care of a baby for about four hours in the morning, do Tae Kwon Do practice in the afternoon, go to the office, and do interviews. I don't really see that many people who are outside the business except for the karate people.

*Have you noticed
that certain fans have stayed with you
for several years?*

I had never seen any martial arts at all. I didn't even know it existed. I vaguely knew about karate, but it was way off in the distance. I had never seen anybody do it. Then I saw a bunch of Bruce Lee movies. He was referred to as the best technician there was. It was just appalling to watch the guy move. It was like a

How did you get started with Karate?

Grace Slick / 155

ballet. It was so impressive, I thought I might have to try and learn it.

It's difficult to learn. Your body has to be in really good shape. It's taxing. But the better shape your body is in, the better shape your brain is in. That's really it.

I've never seen a sport that employs the entire body, mind and spirit. I find that they've gotten rid of a lot of extraneous junk. In this country, they're trying to separate religion and sport from self-conduct. It's all sort of a hodgepodge, it's all separated. Martial arts is not designed just to kick people's faces in. It's training for bodies and minds and concentration. It's not purely to knock people around.

There are a lot of different styles. I don't know much about judo yet, but I've seen a couple of exhibitions, and I'm not too fond of it because they mostly pull each other around by the shirt. It seems like you ought to get your body in shape and be able to pull somebody down catlike rather than dragging them around by the shirt. When I was a teenager, we used to have slumber parties, and we used to wear pajamas. That's what we used to do, drag each other around by the shirt. Judo looked like a slumber party to me. It didn't look like very much use of the body.

Tae Kwon Do is a very beautiful sport to watch. It makes you feel great, and they really work us out, too. They run us through the grinder, I'm just wringing wet when I get through. It makes you feel really good. If you're going to go into tournament karate, then that's all you do. I make music and do other stuff too, and have a kid, and I can't practice nine hours a day at it, which is what you would have to do it you're really going to be good. So it takes a longer time this way. I don't work out every day, I go every other day, or three days a week hopefully. That way it takes a longer time to build the body up into good shape which is having a good sense of balance, and muscles which are able to do what they are supposed to do without getting sore. Paul is going, too, and we're both a little sloppy at the moment.

Do you think Karate will end up replacing drugs for you?

Oh yes, it's a lot cheaper than cocaine, and it gets you really high. If you stand in the middle of the floor and tense every single muscle in your body for five seconds, including your face, then growl, and bring your face way back away from your cheeks, all of a sudden you're just sort of wired after you get through doing it. That's what they sometimes do before they start a fight, they tense every muscle in their bodies. It's like taking a snort of cocaine or snuff or getting a shot of methedrine. But it's better than that because it goes away and you don't have to come down. I don't like the feeling of coming down from methedrine. I'd rather come down from myself. And it's legal. I didn't like it at all as a kid, but it's really fun. Since I'd never done it, I didn't realize how much fun it is to just move your body like crazy for a couple of hours.

Yes, they are from what I've seen. We haven't played live for quite some time, so I don't know how they are as far as reacting to us. But they seem to have changed because the country is in a mess. There are more kids who are taking downers and getting drunk and they have no spirit because there is no spirit to look forward to. It's a little hard on them to get excited about anything. It's hard for them to even get the gas to get anywhere.

How do you think audiences have changed since you first starting performing? Do you think that they are different now?

Oh yes. We want to start doing it again sometime, try and form some kind of screwball band. Jack and Jorma are in Europe and so Paul and I are going to try to get a bunch of people together to fool around and see what happens.

Do you miss performing live?

I'm pleased with the way it came out. I like Spanish music, so it turned out sort of half-assed Spanish, and rock and roll, and there is one tune that is kind of like an old barroom Mae West song, and one song that has bagpipes on it. But one side is sort of that half-assed Spanish. I'm not nuts about the Spanish government, but I do like their music.

It's really fun when someone says, OK you get to do an album of your own in a way you want to. That's why I did one whole side straight through, without any cuts on it. I wanted to use an orchestra, so part of some of it has orchestra. It was really fun to do it. For the guy who did the orchestrations, it was the first time he'd ever led an orchestra, and it was the first time I've ever sung with one, so it's a little loose, because we really didn't know exactly what we were doing. Parts of it though are very nice.

How do you feel about your new album?

I imagine they have. I don't think there is any way you can get around that. If you get on a stage and have more or less of your own personality, then they are more or less correct. I am close to the way they see me. I think they see me as being a little icy, sort of rowdy, a bit sarcastic. That's pretty much the way I am. They're pretty close.

Do you think the press has created an image for you? How do you feel about it?

Grace Slick / 157

**Do you think
the music business is lonely?**

Oh no, not at all. I like to spend time in my room all by myself, so I don't get lonely. I like being alone sometimes, so I don't notice that. I know Janis did, she felt lonely. That old thing about being lonely in a crowd. She kind of felt like she was all by herself in a room full of eighty people. But when I'm in a room full of eighty people, I feel like I'm in a room full of eighty people. It drives me crazy.

How does that affect your privacy?

I don't have any problems about privacy. Every house I move into, I get a lock on the door to my room, otherwise I go bats. I like to have a piano in there, and my drawing things. I get up in the morning early with China, and sort of stay up late at night so I usually take naps. I go in there and nap and fool around, maybe do some sewing, draw, fool around with the piano, whatever I feel like doing at the time.

**Is it hard to
reconcile being in the music business
and taking care of a baby?**

Yes, sometimes I do feel it is, but not to the point of going crazy. It is a little bit peculiar at times. It's more or less what I've been taught, and the matter of being polite to the girl who takes care of China. In other words, I would like to go out a lot, but that sort of means she can't go out. Sometimes I feel guilty about the fact that she's got to always stay around at home. That's sort of a problem. I don't like to do it, but I do it anyway. I kind of go out anyway, and then I think, oh, I shouldn't have done it. You're taught that the mother is always supposed to be with the baby. That's what I was taught. So I feel that. But China is growing up and getting very bright being around so many different kinds of people. She doesn't have to just listen to my style of personality. She gets to hear from five or six different adults who are around her every day. She goes to our parties and she goes to the studio, and she's learning by not being around just one person, so there's actually a benefit in it.

**How do you feel
about the music business now?**

Right now everybody I talk to is sort of in a period of going from one position to another. Everybody wants to do something different. They want to go out on the road and do something new. Write some new music. It's hard for most of us to figure out what to do because the country is so messy. It's hard to even give people hope. Now I could say communism, but that gags about 40 million people. It just depends on the way you look at it. It's hard to keep singing songs like "I love you baby, and I wish you'd come back to me." I can't do that because I've already heard it, everybody's heard it. Everybody I've talked to feels that way, they want to sing about something new. They are in transition, moving from one end of music to another.

I think as you grow, or just by living, you find new things to be interested in. Each individual finds new things. Paul will all of a sudden get interested in a new subject and he writes about that. I got interested in Spanish stuff so I wrote about that. Jorma finds he likes speed skating so maybe he'll write a song about Amsterdam. So you change constantly. The music changes with it. If you're a popular singer, you sing about what you're doing.

How do you think
The Airplane's music has changed
over the past few years?

It's only affected me negatively. It's affected other women positively, I know. They suddenly feel better about pushing. They feel yes, gee, I am wonderful, I didn't realize that before, I thought I was a piece of shit before. But for me, I've worked since I was eighteen and I have kind of a, well, violent personality. Before, people thought, well that's just Grace. Now guys are inclined to think, oh, she's being women's lib at me, you know, being mad at man. I'm not ever mad at any men. So all it's done to me is kind of botch things up. Where they used to think it was just old feisty Grace, now some of them think I'm slamming men, which I'm not. So it hasn't done anything for me.

I never noticed the things that everyone seems to be complaining about, like women being treated like dummies. I really haven't noticed it, either that or I'm too stupid to notice it.

Also rock and roll sounds like big macho stuff, but musicians generally don't treat women badly. I think businessmen are more inclined to act that way. I've noticed that business guys are aloof and treat you as if you were some kind of a pretty little animal. But musicians usually don't. They are generally pretty straight with everybody.

Has the woman's movement
affected you at all?

Well, some of those. Not too many, though. I mean guys who are accountants or salesmen or bankers, mainly because they don't work with women. Musicians do work with women a lot, as publicists, singers. They're used to it. Whereas businessmen have women around them whose only function is as secretaries, do-this, do-that roles. So they have a different attitude. The women who are complaining may be right, it's just that I have never been in that situation, so I don't have anything to be pissed off about. I'm just not in that kind of structure.

When you refer to businessmen,
do you mean record-company people?

The biggest contribution was the fact that I lived on Market Street when I was a kid, and if you live on a four-lane freeway-type street, then you tend to do things inside, like piano and drawing. I'd never

What elements do you think
contributed most to your feeling of
wanting to be creative?

Grace Slick / 159

done any sports. Karate is the first sport I've ever liked. Western sports to me always looked like everybody was just bashing their heads together. There was nothing catlike or graceful about them. Boxing looked clumsy, football looked like a bunch of guys knocking their heads together. I was never interested in any sports and I never got started in any because you can't play on a four-lane highway. So what I did was play inside. Most of the stuff I do is the result of living on a big street.

Do you think there is any conflict involved in being a woman singing rock and roll?

It is kind of masculine, and some women are a little bit more masculine than others. I'm probably one of them. Some guys are more laid back and some men are more aggressive. It seems natural to me because I'm sort of aggressive anyway I'm like that off stage, too. It's the same with the way I dress. I dress up Japanese, sometimes I dress in Levi's, sometimes in a long dress with a lot of spangles on it, sometimes Spanish. I dress up sometimes and act like someone out of a story I read when I was little. The all-beige look bores my facial hairs.

Do you have any specific career goals?

Yes, I'd like to get back into movies someday, eventually. I called my album *Theme From the Movie Manhole.* There is no movie "Manhole," but I like soundtracks so I called it that anyway. I figured, well, I don't have a movie, but I'll make a soundtrack anyway. I'd like to do soundtracks, and do acting in movies, and animation and drawing. All that.

How do you feel about marriage now?

When I was three I decided I would be married in Grace Cathedral, because that's my name, and I was. I've already done that. The only reason now that Paul and I would get married is because of the government. It couldn't possibly change anything except that our taxes would go down. I only 'think of marriage in terms of the government.

Do you think you are happy now?

Oh yes. I think everybody, unless you're seriously ill, is happy in and out. Some days are good and some days are bad. Things seem to be pretty normal.

ALICE STUART

The cover of Alice Stuart's first album for Fantasy Records, *Full Time Woman*, presented her leaning down from the seat of a large black motorcycle to plant a kiss on a small boy. The photographs on the rear of the jacket showed her underneath a head of zapped-out blonde hair, in a leather jacket and some rather ragged duds. I had a hunch Alice wasn't kidding.

As it turned out, the pictures didn't tell the whole story. The young boy was her son, and the record revealed a soft, feminine voice singing some fine original songs. But yet, not the entire picture. At a subsequent appearance at the Ash Grove in Los Angeles, Alice Stuart stood behind an electric guitar and played solid lead rock and roll. I must admit I was surprised, and pleased.

An interesting transition has taken place. From her first album for Arhoolie Records, *All the Good Times*, in which she took a specifically folk-oriented focus, Alice has progressed through the *Full Time Woman* period to her current style. Together with drummer Bob Jones and bass player Ken Severeid, she is Alice Stuart and Snake, a rock trio with warmth and vitality, dedicated to good times and audience enjoyment. They are able to interpret not only Alice's compositions but those of classic blues, rock and progressive country writers.

At the same time, Alice has softened her personal outlook. At thirty-one, her demeanor now is one of calm and grace. Even on stage while she is playing at her most energetic, Alice maintains an ironically gentle mein. She is concerned now with the way she dresses, the image she projects. The effect is most appealing and inimitable. She is able to win over a hypercritical San Francisco Winterland audience and earn praise in print as "a superb guitarist." This is no novelty. Alice Stuart is a talented guitar player capable of writing very good songs. Recently, she has been focusing on her voice, perhaps her weak link, and has been studying with a vocal coach for over two years.

Alice came to Fantasy Records at the time that Creedence Clearwater Revival was on its way to becoming one of the top groups in the country. The label was hot, doing a good deal of recording, and Alice was playing guitar on sessions for Lenny Williams, later to become lead singer for Tower of Power, and Billie J. BeCoat. She was encouraged to perform her own material, and two albums followed, *Full Time Woman*, and *Believing*. But things did not work out as planned. Business conflicts developed and began to occupy more and more of her time. Unfortunately, much of her time at Fantasy was spent trying to get out of her contract. The lessons are valuable ones and the situation all too familiar. Names can be interchanged any number of times with the same results.

In mid-1973, she finally broke her recording contract, and started concentrating on performing in the northern California area. Growing popularity encouraged her and by the beginning of 1974 Alice Stuart and Snake had a large, enthusiastic audience. Unfortunately, in February, the guitar she had spent three years adjusting to her specific needs, the one she refers to in the following interview, was stolen from her in Berkeley. For Alice, a major setback, and one that will take time and energy to mend.

It's been a long road from Alice's hometown of Lake Chelan, Washington. She is now looking forward to starting again with a new guitar and a new record label. As her audience grows, the hopes are that her dues have been paid in full.

I grew up in a little town in Washington State, Lake Chelan. I started playing the piano when I was five or six, and I played the drums. I started writing songs pretty early, too. When I graduated from high school, I got a baritone ukelele, which is very much like a tenor guitar. It's supposed to be tuned like a ukelele, but I tuned it like the top four strings of the guitar. Then about a year later, I did get a "real" guitar.

I figure I started playing guitar seriously in 1962. I played for about a year in Seattle and then I went down to Los Angeles and tried to get into the scene down there. But I just didn't fit in. It was about 1964 and the Ash Grove was the big folk club. I remember Taj Mahal was playing there, he was just coming up. But I just didn't fit into the scene, even though I tried my damndest.

Then a friend of mine, Paul Hansen, a folk singer and part-time actor, contacted Barry Olivier, who put on the Berkeley Folk Festival, and told him that he should come down and meet me and see me play. That's how I ended up in the Berkeley Folk Festival. All of a sudden, after playing guitar for only about two years or so, I was thrown into the company of people like Pete Seeger and Joan Baez. I couldnt believe it. I felt that I didn't deserve it. I felt somehow I missed the middle of "the climb up."

Then I was told that I should make a record, so I did an album for Arhoolie Records. It was my first one. I felt that I was a good picker, but I really didn't know what the fuck I was doing.

Then I was sent on tour to the East Coast. I went for six months and, at the time, I had no confidence in myself at all. I was playing guitar, banjo, and autoharp and performed all by myself. I didn't do any of my own tunes, I did all folk stuff and a lot of Dylan material. Some nights I would just be awful and other nights I would be great. But I couldn't be consistent because I had no idea what made me great and what made me terrible. Sometimes right in the middle of a set, I would start to cry. I would have to leave the stage.

I was so lonely that I came home and met this guy on Telegraph Avenue in Berkeley. I took him home and fed him chocolate chip cookies and married him a couple of weeks later. That really helped my head out a lot. He had been places I had never been. I was very sheltered, even though I didn't think I was when I was young. I did all those things like sneaking out at night, but I was actually very sheltered in that I really didn't know about the hardness of life. I think it's because I was raised in such a small town. The things that go on in cities still mystify me, but at least I'm old enough now to grasp it a little bit.

Anyway, I took a year and a half break and had my baby, my little boy who's seven now. Then when I got back into music, for some reason the confidence was there. My son helped a lot. I learned a lot of things. Plus his father helped me. I had never taken acid. I couldn't smoke grass. I just got crazy every time I'd smoke grass. I drank a little but not very much. I was very straight.

Every time I would start to get real crazy with him and do weird things, he would open my mouth and throw acid down my throat and make me take it. I hated him for it at the time, but if it hadn't been for him, I really don't think I would have ever gotten it together. He really helped me an amazing amount.

Then I was in the first Sky River Rock Festival in Seattle. That was my coming out thing pretty much. It was my getting back into music after being out of it for a long time. I played acoustic guitar, again performing by myself. From there I left my husband and took my son up to Vancouver and played in a club up there for a while.

When I got back to Berkeley, I had to go on welfare. I was on welfare for a year and I taught guitar for $10 an hour when I could. Within a year's time I had it together enough to start writing again after about a ten-year lapse. I don't know what happened to me, I just all of a sudden started writing again.

I was also doing session work for Fantasy Records, playing guitar on other people's records. A producer heard me and asked if I did anything on my own, if I sang. So I sang him all this folk music and he said, "I don't want to hear that shit, I want to hear your own things."

I told him that I never sang them for anybody, that I just wrote them and put them aside, which I did. Finally we made a demo, and they liked it so I was signed to Fantasy. It was a year to the month after I had gone on welfare, and I could finally put an end to that.

I got three bands together before I ended up with the band I have now. We've been together about three years. You know I think back on that first Fantasy album, *Full Time Woman*, and I've changed my mind about it. I'm much happier with it now than I was when it first came out. The musicians I work with now weren't on it, but I do believe that it was where I was at the time, and that it was done as well as it could have been with the equipment we had to work with. We had an eight-track machine with no board. Everything was a wreck. There was nothing you could do to the sound. It just came in direct, so when you mixed the sound there was no way you could get any presence. If it wasn't recorded right in the first place, there was nothing you could do.

The musicians were getting $15 a session. It didn't matter how long the sessions lasted, either. If it was a seven-hour session, they still got $15. When Richard Greene, the violin player, came in, I told my producer, "You make out an actual W2 on this cat because he's getting paid union scale. Period." Everybody in the whole place threw a fit, but I was finally getting some balls. I didn't have any confidence before that, so I couldn't say things. The president of the company told me he didn't think we needed anybody that professional on the album. I told him I thought we did.

The guy who produced that album is a cat named Jesse Osborne. I really didn't realize for a long time how good he was and how sensitive he was to my music. I feel badly that I put him down in interviews that I did then. People asked me questions and I would say that he was a black producer who was into rhythm and blues and who wanted to make me into something different. But he didn't want to make me into anything other than who I really *was*, and it could be that I didn't know who I was as well as he did.

We would have these fights that would last for two weeks and I would refuse to come to the studio because he would hurt my feelings. He would say, "Put down that goddam guitar and sing." In a way he was right, and in a way he was wrong. He didn't realize that I'm a guitar player as well as a singer.

Now I take voice lessons. I've been studying with Judy Davis for almost three years, and I think she's the best. Barbra Streisand flies out here from New York to go to her. She teaches a lot of different kinds of singers, as well as helping actors with things like projection. She's helped me immensely because now I can be up for three days and still sing, and nobody knows the difference. Before, even if I'd gotten a regular amount of sleep, I still couldn't be consistent. Now I can. I can do almost anything to myself and still do it.

I think you almost have to be better. You can't be average. To tell you the truth, I never really related to myself as a woman on a playing level. I just couldn't. I can't wear skirts when I play. I can't do it because I feel so uncomfortable, and I feel like people might be

Do you think things have been harder for you professionally because you are a woman?

emphasizing something else besides the music. Plus, how the fuck can you bend over and fix your amplifier and stuff in a skirt? How can you feel right about that?

People have asked me that question before, and it's really a hard one, because I'm sure I've felt it, but I've never looked at it that way. I feel that whoever you are, you do get what you deserve. If you earn it. I used to get mad when people didn't like me or they said I played pretty good guitar for a chick. They hardly ever say that to me anymore, but I used to play pretty good for a chick and how can I put somebody down for saying that? It wasn't forceful enough. Now I really play.

No, I don't think it's been any harder. Maybe it has helped me. Lots of cats will let things slide, I think. Or they can have a backup guitar player. But with me, I've always wanted to be a player. I was going to give up singing entirely because it was putting me so uptight. I felt like I had to be so good, try to stop smoking all the time and not drink, not stay up that late. I can play when I'm just totaled, it doesn't matter. But singing is a dedicated thing. There are few singers in rock and roll as far as I'm concerned who honest to God get up there and try to produce a tone that is pleasant to listen to. It's one of my goals. If I'm going to do it, I'm going to do it well, or I'm not going to do it at all.

What made you switch to electric guitar?

I always wanted to play electric music, always. But when I first picked up the guitar, the in thing was folk music. I picked up an electric guitar when I came back to Berkeley from Vancouver in about 1968 or '69. I felt people were going to laugh at me. That's the only thing I felt. I didn't feel that "nobody plays electric guitar." I felt people were going to laugh at me, which they did. It was a little difficult that way, because the people who came to see me play were my old fans from the folk days and they were just horrified. They thought it was tasteless. But I did it anyway because I had to do what made me happy.

I had gone as far as I wanted to go with acoustic guitar. I could play it in my sleep, and I didn't care about it any more. Electric guitar keeps growing and growing because there are so many more possibilities with it.

For instance, you can work up the neck. Acoustic guitar is made basically as a chordal instrument. You can pick things on it, but it's mosly first position stuff on the lower frets. It doesn't blend with electric instruments on stage as far as I'm concerned unless it's an acoustic guitar with a built in pick-up. But I just didn't like the feel of an acoustic guitar. I never did. I had to fight it every inch of the way.

My electric guitar just bends with me. I spent three years setting it up the way I have to have it. Using the right type of strings, getting

the bridge right, getting everything exactly set up for me. I can do it myself, too. With an acoustic guitar, you have to take it into a shop and depend on somebody else to do it. You're constantly battling with it, constantly fighting it. I could never stand real thin strings on an acoustic because then you get that light, dumb, ethereal sound. On my electric guitar, I have very light strings on top because it's a subtle, gentle sound, plus I do a good deal of bending on the top strings. I have heavy strings on the bottom because I want to be hard on them. If you used a set of strings like that on an acoustic, you'd have to have the whole instrument rearranged. It's just time consuming and if you don't know how to do it yourself, you're lost.

What are your musical references? What types of music have influenced you?

The first music I recall hearing was from the '40s, "Embraceable You" and tunes like that. There was a woman who lived in the house where I lived, who used to play piano. She played all those songs, ones like "Sentimental Me." I would sit and listen to her play and I would cry.

My mother didn't live at home. She worked out and I lived with my aunt. My mother would come home at Christmas and other times for a week or so and she loved country music. I hated it with a passion and thought it was just awful, but when my own style came out, country was in there, too.

I listened to Jerry Lee Lewis, Little Richard, Buddy Holly. I listened to a lot of early Johnny Cash. I used to write rock and roll songs when I was about fourteen or fifteen years old. I tried to sing them for high school assemblies, but I was so paranoid about my voice. I knew I needed help even then, but my aunt wouldn't send me to a voice teacher. I just couldn't get the sound out, but at least I tried.

I played classical music on the piano, but I played it my way, which infuriated the people who were teaching me. They'd tell me, "That's not the way it was written, can't you read this?" I honest to God didn't care. I liked the way I played better.

Do you feel you have to be sexy on stage?

There was a conflict for a while because I absolutely refused to do anything like that. I would just wear whatever I wanted to wear and that was it. But at this point, I feel very confident in what I do, I like what I do, and I think that the audience gets warmer when I try to dress in a way that says, "Yes I am a woman, but no I'm not a sex symbol." For one thing, because it makes me feel good.

Finally I'm up to the point where I can wear clothes I think look good on me and also display the fact that I am a woman. But that feeling is very new, maybe six months, maybe a year old.

For our first gig at Winterland, we planned for two weeks so we would look good together on stage as a unit. I think about that kind of thing now because I feel we've got the music together enough to think about the clothes. I hate it when people get all their money trips together, they get all their equipment and their clothes together, but they can't play. I don't believe in doing it backwards. We're into that now. We try to look as good as we can.

How do you feel about the music business?

It's dog eat dog. No, seriously, I love the excitement of it. I was born to live like this. I feel that in order to stay above some of the jive things that happen you have to really think a lot unless you want to be led around by the nose. I think my lack of confidence helped me because I was always beneath everyone else as far as I was concerned. So I was never able to let anybody push me beyond what I thought I could do. At this point I can make my own decisions and I do what I want to do when I want to do it. It has come to the point now where my manager and I get together and we talk about what should happen next, and two weeks, a month later, it happens. To me, that means that we have got a pretty good idea of realistically where we're at. I don't think too many groups do.

Record companies, I know why they're in it. They're in it to make money. They stand to make a lot more money than the artist does. They always do. Right now I try not to accept right off what somebody might tell me. For instance, the president of Fantasy told me, "Oh yes, we've got all the confidence in the world in you and we just think you're going to make it and we're going to do everything we can to push you." OK. Everything they could except put money into it. He loaned me money a lot of times for this and that, speakers and stuff. But I mean promotional money. There was one ad for *Full Time Woman*, and that was in *Rolling Stone* and that's because I bitched and screamed and jumped up and down. A half-page ad. Once.

I believe they didn't know they were treating me unfairly. I believe that they were innocent. I believe that I hurt the president of the company because in his own way he was behind me and did believe in me.

I went to him time and time again and told him that he had to come and see us play, to give us a little bit of feeling that our record company really did care. Frankly, they didn't like my band. They didn't want me to have a band. They wanted me to be like Melanie or something. And I went in for a year and told them to come and give us a little confidence. We gave them complete lists of where we would be playing.

We were invited to be on the Dick Cavett Show and we needed money to get there and he locked his door and said he wouldn't come up with any more money. For the Dick Cavett Show? George Carlin was the guest host and he called me personally to be on the show. He didn't know me, he had just heard the album and loved it. We finally got the money to go. We had to borrow it. When I got there I told George not to mention the record company at all. I told him he could show the album if he wanted to, but I asked him not to mention Fantasy at all.

That was it for me. I had been telling everybody that the record company meant well, that they would come through for us, but when the Cavett thing happened, I gave up. I went to my lawyer and said, "I want out." That was in January 1972.

Do you think that kind of behavior is indicative of what's going on in the music business?

No, I think Fantasy ought to be a French laundry. I'll tell you what they do best, they put out jazz best. You can't push jazz. You just press it and put it in a nice package and put it in the stores. I don't think they ever knew what to do with rock and roll. Not even with Creedence. They signed Creedence to a ten-year contract and the group can't get out of it. John Fogerty spent a lot of money on lawyers, too, but nothing worked. It's ironclad.

How do you feel about the music scene?

That is a disillusionment to me a lot of times. There are some people I really respect as artists who, as people, well they're not empty-headed, they just don't know how to be people. They're so busy trying to be musicians and put up a front, be cool, it's all such a cool game that they can't get down with you. I used to figure they were like that to me because I was nowhere. But of late I've found out they're like that because they can't help themselves.

That is another reason I'm glad it's been a slow, steady climb for me, because I think I've gained a personality that's really me. This is the way I really am, but I had to get some confidence before I could feel this way.

Are you the same person off stage as you are on stage?

Yes, finally. I used to be terrified, too, every time I would play. Not any more. For one thing, taking voice lessons gives you confidence to know that even if you might not sound as you sounded the night before, you can do it because you know the mechanics. Also, if I don't play guitar enough I get a little paranoid that I'm not going to play right, but it doesn't last long, or I'll immediately make a joke about it. I will say something and then the feeling of paranoia will just go away, because to me honesty always wins out. There are very few people who know that and believe it.

Very few times have I bumped into people who are just as real off stage as they are on stage. When I'm on stage, I'm a little flashier. Sometimes I get very shy off stage.

How does rock and roll affect your personal life?

Oh man, that's a very good question. I find it's very hard for cats to accept what I do. I find it very hard. Why can't they understand that it is just my gig, like whatever they do is their gig?

I just had a scene with this cat. I thought it was together and that he would be able to deal with it. All of a sudden after two or three weeks he turned on me. I made one decision and he said, "well, you're the leader of the band. I guess you're just used to making heavy decisions all by yourself. You don't need me." He just got weird. That's what happens.

If chicks have an old man who sings and plays, they are usually proud of it. It doesn't work that way with men when women are on stage. It should, but it doesn't. I guess you could call it being threatened, but it makes no sense to me. It's hard for me to be with a guy, and it's very hard for me to be without a guy, too, because I have a seven-year-old son and he digs having men around, too. But the way it is now, it's just like a day at a time. I can't even think seriously, especially after this last scene.

I really liked the guy. As it turned out, he was more interested in the possibility of making some money off me. When I found that out it shattered me. It made me think about what might happen when I'm making $5,000 a night, because this guy had me snowed. I believed every word he told me, and I didn't think I was like that. I'm not that naive. He was just real smooth. He'd been with me for two weeks and all of a sudden he wanted his name on the business cards.

I finally said, "Can't you just be my old man?" When that happened, it was all over. Since we've kind of broken it off, I've heard from a couple of people who know him well that if the money wasn't happening, he wouldn't be around very long. That's exactly what happened. Isn't that awful? And I think, well now, when I start making money, how am I going to know if a cat's really real? I've never been fooled like that.

Do you think rock and roll is a lonely business?

Yes I do. I think any kind of art is lonely, any kind of music, not just rock and roll. Maybe folk music is less lonely because people get together and pick and don't care much about the professional part of it. But any professional type of music is lonely.

Alice Stuart / 173

How do you feel about traveling?

I love it. Every time I get a chance to go on tour, I love it. But coming off a trip, especially if it's a long one, is like coming down for me. I cry when I come home. I'm down for three, four, five days. It's like getting really loaded and then coming down.

What kind of an image do you think you have?

At this point, I think I have a wholesome image, but I also have a very independent, non-wimpy image. People usually don't think that I'm trying to do more than I can do.

I've never been pretty in my life until maybe the last year, because I was never happy with who I was. The image I project I think is pretty much how I feel about myself. I feel better about myself now than I ever have in my life. As far as I'm concerned, my music and my life are one and the same. If my music is going well, then I'm learning, I'm progressing.

I also have two of the best people to work with that I've ever run across anywhere, the most dedicated and some of the best musicians there are. They're the ones who have actually given me the confidence to go ahead and play. They never came on to me like a chick, they came on to me like a musician. Our group is really a shared experience.

Is it hard for you to win an audience?

It used to be hard, but it isn't any more because it's easier for me to feel out what they want to hear. It's easier for me to be confident in what I want to give them. At this point, I know how to get their attention. All you have to do with an audience, usually, is give them what you know is going to get them off first, and then you give them something that is yours personally and that's from your heart, and they've got to dig it. It's not hard any more, but it used to be very difficult for me.

Was it difficult because you surprised people being a woman playing lead electric guitar?

Well, it was partially that, but it wouldn't have surprised them so much if I'd have been a little better at it before. I've just gotten good enough at it that nobody has to pay any attention to it anymore. At this point people can listen to the music and not be preoccupied with the fact that it's a woman playing lead. When people first hear the music lots of times, they don't realize it, especially if Bob, the drummer, is singing when somebody walks in. Sometimes they don't even notice, which is what I've always tried to do. That's why I never got mad at people who said, "You play pretty good for a chick," because that meant my guitar and I were not together yet.

174 / Alice Stuart

That meant that we were two separate things and now I don't feel that way. It's just like my voice, well, I mean I'm not that good yet, but I'm to the point where people don't think about it.

How would you describe your music?

I would describe it as an amalgam of every kind of music I've ever heard or enjoyed or listened to, everything from rhythm and blues to classical, country, blues. Most of it is basically happy music. We've added an awful lot of things to our repertoire to get an audience in particular clubs. You have to keep them going constantly.

Do you feel you're struggling?

I did until the first Winterland gig came through. We got such good reviews and promises of repeat shows. Things seem to be coming through for us again. I don't feel that we're downtrodden. I don't feel that we're paying dues that we shouldn't be paying. I feel that everybody gets what they deserve when they deserve it. I've never felt like we weren't getting what we deserved. Or that I wasn't.

Do you think becoming very successful will change you at all?

No, I don't think it will do anything except make me a little more comfortable. That's what I was talking about earlier, about watching these people who don't even know how to drive a car and turn left unless they've got somebody sitting next to them and telling them to turn left. Some people don't pick the right people to direct them. Some people pick managers who don't understand that you can't promote everyone the same way. My manager and I talk things out, he makes some decisions and I make some decisions, and we make decisions together. But he doesn't tell me to do something that would be completely against who I am. He knows me too well. And we wouldn't bring anybody into this organization who wasn't like that.

Are you sacrificing anything for your career?

Yes. I wish I had more time to give my son, mostly. But I will have. I will have when I have a little more money and we don't have to work five nights a week at dumb little gigs, I'll have more time. That's the main thing I think I'm sacrificing.

What do you like best about what you do?

The actual performance. I really enjoy it. I wish I had more time to write, though, because I really enjoy that too. Right now I just don't have time to create as much as I'd like to because we're working too much.

Yes, that happens a lot. A lot of chicks come up to me and ask me, in fact it used to piss me off I must say, they'd say, "How does it feel being a chick playing guitar?" The minute that I would hear that remark, I would just want to hit them. Because I figure if that's your attitude, then you're going to be chick playing guitar and you're not going to be a guitar player. I think I've been the cause of a lot of chicks actually seriously taking up electric guitar. I just wish their attitudes with it were different. I wish they would think of themselves first as musicians.

Do women come up to you and tell you that you've encouraged them to play electric guitar? To seriously pursue rock and roll?

WENDY WALDMAN

One of the most impressive debut albums of 1973 came from Wendy Waldman, a young Los Angeles-based musician. Wendy is a singer-songwriter of wit and perceptiveness, able to weave her feelings into accessible lyric and melody equations. She sounds a bit like Laura Nyro without the melodramatic inflection, and reminds some of Joni Mitchell in her attention to detail and her desire to mold songs into complete and clearly defined statements.

A larger measure of her musical talent comes naturally, inherited from her family. Her grandfather was a composer, and her father, Fred Steiner, is also a noted writer-arranger. He has done a good deal of work for television, and his credits include the theme music for programs as diverse as "Perry Mason," and episodes for "Star Trek" and "Bullwinkle."

Wendy began to think seriously of a musical career before she graduated from high school. She likes to refer to "de blooze" and "de jug band music," as two of her favorite areas of music, the spoken reference a gesture of affection. Her first jug band was assembled at Oakwood School, a private high school in the San Fernando Valley area of Los Angeles, where she met her husband, Ken Waldman. He was teaching one of her eleventh-grade courses and the jug band was both a good excuse for them to see each other, as well as way for Wendy to pursue her musical interests. As Diamond Roscoe's Jubilee Quintet, the group recorded "Chauffeur Blues," and "Salty Dog," with Ken producing and Wendy on vocals, guitar and kazoo.

Early experimentation with the jug band idiom led to the formation of a more serious group, called Bryndle, which was signed to A&M Records for a time. Although produced by both Chuck Plotkin and then Lou Adler, Bryndle never released any material, and the group disbanded. Finally, Wendy became a solo performer. Reunited with her original producer, Chuck Plotkin, she began, with the help of friends and family, to put together an album which consumed two years of effort. It was three-quarters finished before Warner Brothers decided it was worth a calculated gamble. Warners paid for the rest of the production costs, and Wendy's debut, *Love Has Got Me*, emerged. It proved tightly arranged and remarkably consistent, considering that it was recorded piecemeal, during off-hours when other, more financially solvent musicians were not at work.

The album was a deeply personal effort by Wendy, who taught herself to read and write music so that she could do her own arrangements (with the exception of two tunes which were arranged by her father). She is now studiowise, and through her family experience and her business acumen, she is also music industrywise as well.

On stage, Wendy still shows a degree of inexperience, which is soon overshadowed by a genuine enthusiasm for her chosen craft. Signs of hesitancy and awkwardness gradually recede as songs progress. She will admit that she is in a learning process, yet there are moments on stage when flashes of professional brilliance override that impression.

Wendy enjoys looking flashy during her performances, dressing up and moving lithely under an extraordinary thatch of dark electric hair which she leaves unfettered as she sings and plays both piano and guitar. She also sometimes projects a level of self-confidence which has been interpreted on more than one occasion as arrogance. The fact that she demands thorough concentration and clear leadership from her band adds to this suggestion, yet this, too, can be a strength. She has an awareness of her talent and what she intends to do with it.

"It is important to write," she says, "but it is equally important to sing." Wendy Waldman feels no pressures to defer her outlook, a point of view already captured in exceptionally well-written songs. With the strength of her convictions, her rise in the industry should prove equally well defined.

How did you get together with your producer, Chuck Plotkin? You mentioned that your first album was two years in the making. Why did it take so long?

Well, I was working in a little slop house down in Venice, California, called The Attica, playing "de blooze" and serving up food. Chuck was a young, soon to be lawyer. He would come in on the weekends like all the young lawyers, with their good-looking women, and have a bottle of wine and exquisite food, really fine food. And we played music. At that time The Attica was in its heyday, and only the very best musicians would play there. A lot of people who have gone on to bigger and better things would play there.

I was eighteen at the time and very cool. I guess I had a kind of "leave me alone" attitude. Chuck would come around. He was a musician and he already had been working with Steve Ferguson on an album for Asylum. Chuck used to tell me that I was great and that he loved my music. I used to think he was hustling me. Six months later, he was still coming in. It got to be really nice to see him. Finally he came out to the house.

He still had money in those days. This was before he seriously got into music. The day he was supposed to take his bar exam, the rest of us were up at Big Sur, at Esalen, playing at this incredible little country music festival. He didn't go to the festival, but I know he didn't take his bar exam. He just dropped out to manage us, us being Bryndle, a six-piece, six-part vocal band with myself, Kenny Edwards, Carla Bonoff, Andrew Gold, and later Peter Bernstein and Dennis Wood.

Wendy Waldman / 183

We were signed to A&M but it didn't exactly work out. We learned that we didn't want to make records with some guy telling us, "This time is costing you $100 an hour. You only have fifteen minutes before this session is over, and this is not a hit record." Bryndle was an excellent band, we were just very young. A&M was good to us, but they didn't have the patience to stay with us. So they had to cut us loose. About eight months later, Chuck had finagled some money and built his own studio, Clover Recorders.

The studio was completed in January of '72 and I went in and started cutting. The first round of stuff was done with some of the same people, Kenny and Andrew and Peter. We cut a few things, "Train Song" was one of them. I cut a bunch of things solo and then went back and overdubbed vocals. We did a lot of work through that spring, just kind of on and off. Other people were paying for studio time, so we could only get in when no one was there. We'd have to work on a Saturday maybe from nine to noon, then ten days later from seven to midnight. We didn't have any money, so we used family musicians who happen to be excellent, and who will soon all be stars in their own right, or whatever it is you can become in a depression.

Who was paying the bills? Nobody was paying the bills, there were no bills. As far as engineering went, Robert Appere, who was Bryndle's engineer at A&M, came to be head engineer at Clover, and there was a young trainee, Michael Boshears, whom I detested, he was too cool. The first time Robert left to do some other business, he left me with Michael and I grumbled and grumbled.

I was doing some vocal tracking at the time, and was in the studio maybe eight or nine hours one night. Michael just stayed with me for every second of it to the point where he was reading my mind. He would run the tape back to the place I wanted it before I even said anything. So I never worked with Robert again. I trained Michael and he became my engineer. I was the first full project that he ever did. He's just become superb. I think he's a tremendous engineer. So there was that problem solved.

The studio time was all underground. It was Chuck's studio and we just didn't pay any studio bills. All our friends were playing. What we all decided was that when we sold the album, everybody would get money.

So, sometime in late spring or early summer, we took the album to David Geffen at Asylum, but he didn't go for it. Maybe it was too funky. The rough draft had an early version of "Can't Come In" and "Gringo In Mexico" that have since been recut. It had other things on there that aren't on there now. So we were kind of out in the cold at that point.

Chuck went next to Warner Bros. All this was taking place over months and months. Finally Lenny Waronker at Warners said, "We like it but it's not really finished. We're going to give you $5,000 and you go back in and cut two more things. We know you guys know how to make records, but maybe with a little money you could make better records."

So we had $5,000 and what we could do with that money! Strings and horns and background vocals! They were expecting two tunes and we came back with the whole second side of the album, plus two others. We came back with seven tunes, tracks played by Wilton Felder on bass, Russ Kunkel on drums, Bobbye Hall Porter on hand percussion, Jim Horn and his horn section, David Campbell and the string section, all the arrangements for which I did. A totally lush second side, with Maria Muldaur and various others singing backgrounds. It seems that we finished that somewhere in the spring, and we took it to Warners and it sat. We still weren't signed so we had to negotiate. It came together in pieces and pieces.

Finally, they decided to sign us. They said the album would come out in September of '73 or the next January. I felt like I had had the album for two years, and I didn't want it for another winter. It was over. We were all suffering from the syndrome of "Is it really finished? Can we really let go of it?"

How the album ended was the best story of all. Here it had been two years, really merging into four or five years working up to it. In late July, all of a sudden we realized we had settled on a September 5th release date. I was planning to go to Yucatan, which I canceled. We had two weeks in which to record new material, do the horn arrangements and record them, do the backgrounds, do the leads, mix and master it, sequence the album, shoot the cover photos, and get ready for the fact that it was over. It all happened in two weeks. And the way each thing happened was like the real stroke of fate. We had one shot to do each activity. We had one meeting on what we were going to cut and how we were going to do it, and then we set up the dates in advance. It all happened just as we planned.

I really feel that I know how to make records now. First I did it under A&M's guidance, or misguidance as it were. Lou Adler tried to produce us and I think he did a poor job. He chose our weakest material. I learned a lot from that experience.

Working at Clover, we learned the craft of the studio and we learned how we'd like things to go. When we finally had the money, we knew we were not into doing long indulgent sessions. None of this "keep trying until we get it right."

Did you study music formally?

No. I come from a musical family. My father's a composer, my grandfather was a composer. I was, and evidently I still am, somewhat rebellious, and I didn't get heavily into classical study until recently. It's begun to interest me. But I was always aware of the classics, and aware of orchestral colors. I love Gershwin and Debussy and Ravel and Stravinsky. I was into blues and traditional music. I was a real folk purist way back before Pete Seeger got so popular again. My question was always, "Where did Pete Seeger get that song?" From Washboard Jimmy. Well I want to hear Washboard Jimmy singing it.But music itself has always overridden its categories to me. It it's music, it's music.

Chuck convinced me that my music was really orchestral and that I should explore those colors. I have an acute ear for an arrangement that satisfies me. When the time came to do arrangements for the album, I felt that I had put all my blood and all my soul into these tracks and into these vocals, it had all been under my control, how could I possibly turn over the string arrangements to some total stranger? The exception was my father, who did two arrangements on the album, and even that was a little strange. I mean how can I get somebody to completely understand a melody that I've already got in my head? I put that to Chuck—big dilemma, Wendy loves a crisis. And he finally said, "Well, in that case, why don't you do it yourself?" That was followed by a small bit of hysterics, "No, no, I can't read music." I had taken a few lessons from my father, but I still didn't think I could do it.

Finally I got so crazy and neurotic about it, I had no choice. I couldn't turn "Waiting For The Rain" over to someone else. I had had that goddamn arrangement in my head from the time I wrote the song.

Finally I talked myself into it. I said to myself, Well, it's not what's on the paper, but it's that you know the notes, so you think about the notes first, decide what you want to hear. Then you can struggle any way you need to, to get it written down. I just forced myself to write those arrangements. First I wrote them in my ears, and then I sat down and charted them on paper. And it turns out I can write music just fine.

When did you think you might want to be a performer?

Well, I've always been a performer. When I was sixteen, we had a jug band, and we played around the city. When I was eighteen, I was working at The Attica. I always knew I would be on some kind of stage from the time I was really young, but I couldn't make it in the young actor's world. It didn't make it for me, I was too soulful or something.

I guess when I was around fourteen, I started singing in little coffee houses. I would sing old Josh White tunes and things like "Summertime."

I went to high school at Oakwood, which is a private school.

That's where I met my husband. He was a teacher there. He had been at Harvard and he knew Jim Kweskin and Geoff and Maria Muldaur and all those people. So he came out to Los Angeles and I was already into "de blooze" at that time. He was teaching some incredibly complex course I had in the eleventh grade. We started a jug band. It was our extracurricular activity, and it was also a good way to see each other because we really liked each other, and he turned me on to a lot of tremendous music.

From the very first time I started to sing, I would notice that I just had a confidence about the fact that I was good, and I would see people's reactions. I would think, this is unusual, this isn't just being a good student. I'm fourteen, and here I am sitting in the Fifth Estate, I've hardly ever sung and here these people are being knocked out by some chick, and I know I'm better than she is. It's not a matter of me being the larger person, but I have a better understanding of my craft.

It was hard to be a folkie in LA in the early '60s, because whoever was a folkie was not about to make room for new people. It was a very tight scene because it was so sparse. I hung out at the Ash Grove quite a bit. I had a jug band and we were damn good.

Do you think
your musical roots are in folk music?

Well, my roots are quite divided actually. My roots are as much in Hollywood film scores and in George Gershwin and Rogers and Hammerstein as they are in Skip James and traditional jug band music and white mountain music. When I was five and six, my sister and I used to sing old white mountain music. We were exposed to a lot of people in the LA underground when we were just little kids. My roots are very broad.

Then I lived in Mexico City for two years. My father was getting into television down there. I was seven years old and it blew me out. I was never the same. My father was still in LA and my mother and sister and I were suddenly in this huge house in Mexico City. We didn't speak the language. The first day of school we were the only kids with no books, because we didn't realize that the book salesman went door to door. We had turned him away, thinking he was just a door-to-door salesman. So people were hassling us in Spanish because we didn't have any books. And we were Jews and that was a little peculiar, although there is a large Jewish community down there. But we were in a primarily Mexican, Turkish, French, German, and American school.

There was more than one occassion when I really had to run for my life. I developed a kind of rebellious attitude. I could run faster. I developed a private little street ethic. All this I just recently came to realize. But the experience of Mexico just blew away forever any notion of being in a peer group. When I came back to LA and all my girlfriends had been wearing their trainer bras and going through their typical young American experience, I had been seeing witches on Lake Patzcuaro, and there really are such things. I'd spent Christmas in Mexico City with firecrackers all over and the strange music and the weird hot food. I had been all around Mexico and I was bizarre from it.

I've just recently become aware that there was a lot of pain in that experience for me. It was also very beautiful. I think it made me able to be whatever it is that I am. I'm grateful.

You said that you have a very specific idea of what your place is as a female in the music business. What is that?

Well, it's more of an attitude toward myself as a female. I've always been this way. I'm the youngest child and that by nature makes me somewhat rebellious. At an early age, I decided that I was not going to be like anybody else. I learned the lesson, and possibly I learned it from my father, that originality and inventiveness in the arts were the most prized. Those are the things to be valued the most.

I was very competitive when I was younger, just in school. What it's turned into now is something different. I'm not a women's libber so it's not an ethic that I carry around. It's a conviction of a personal kind of strength that incorporates my femininity. Until recently, there have not been any women doing what Bonnie Raitt, Linda Ronstadt, me, Maria Muldaur are doing. The kind of struggle that I think Janis must have had to go through to do what she did, I wouldn't have gone through. I decided when I got into the music business, that I was going to know the craft such that I could tell somebody else what I wanted done.

I learned so much in the studio, and my album was as much produced by me as it was by Chuck Plotkin. I chose to arrange ultimately—to learn to arrange on the spot—because I knew that the whole helplessness of chicks in this business is appalling. I've always been fiercely independent about my music. I'm a songwriter and I will try not to write the same song again and again. I intend to move on into composing symphonies of whatever sort.

The same things applies on stage, the helplessness. I have a band of my own and I know how I want them to sound, and if they agree to work with me, I'll work them to the bone until they sound that way. It has paid off. I split my salary equally with them, and whatever my benefits are, their benefits are.

I like to see women get up. And there's no competition between us. It's a funny thing. We work together. Linda Ronstadt and Maria and I all worked on each other's albums. Two of my songs are on Maria's album, I sang on Linda's album, Linda and Maria sang on my album. We were all recording at the same time. There's tremendous love between us.

Wendy Waldman / 189

How do you feel about the music business in general?

The music business is in very serious trouble right now. I love the music business, but there's a depression and it's getting more serious. I hope the function of the depression in the music business is that it will weed out a lot of the bullshit that's been going on. It's a fact that in the last five years or so, the middle class has been turning out guitar players by the droves, seventeen-year-old guitar players. That's not enough, that's not music. I think music has to go back to being a craft. Being a rock and roll star is not necessarily being a musician.

It's a funny thing, because at the time when everything is falling apart, my shit is coming together, which I wonder about. I don't think Warners would have signed me were it today. They signed me months ago and they had to go through with their commitment. I don't think they are going to be sorry about it. They've gotten rid of a lot of their other new artists, but they are going to have to continue to have new blood.

Do you think you've had to work harder because you're a woman?

Yes, definitely. We have a joke in the band that says, "Twenty-five percent off automatically if you're a girl." It started as a very cynical comment from a drummer we had whom we ultimately fired. He really believed that. He hated so much working behind a woman that we had to send him home in the middle of the tour, but we kept the joke. It's a big joke to us.

The way I handled it was that I used to say, If I'm good enough, if I'm really good enough, there's going to be no way that they can deny it. If I'm strong enough in what I have to say, and if my music is righteous enough, they're going to want to hear it too much to bullshit.

A friend of mine always used to say that women can't play rock and roll. They don't have the physical strength and it's just not in their bodies to do it. It used to drive me crazy, because the musicians I played with for years and years were all strong men rock and rollers and I wasn't. I was a blues singer, not a rock and roller. It used to just really kill me.

I remember when I was nineteen, I wouldn't pick up a guitar because I was so hysterical about the fact that I was a chick and I couldn't pull off the trip the way I wanted to. Finally I just decided that was a lie. You must learn to play rock and roll time, you've got to learn to play good rhythm guitar.

Now the problem is that I was not intrinsically a rock and roller. The problem has always been personal, the feeling that I wasn't good enough to satisfy myself. Now I don't worry about it any more.

There's one sort of qualification that I would like to make. I think I can perceive where it's harder to be in this business if you're a chick. I would say that the reason for that is the feeling that you're not good enough to pull off what you do. I wanted to be strong enough in my music so that I could really work with strong people, because there's no point in working with lackadaisical, bullshit musicians.

It has a lot to do with upbringing. When I was eleven, I wanted to play drums and my father said no. Had I played drums, my whole sense of rock and roll would have been different. I wouldn't have had to learn it sort of from the other end. A lot of young rock and roll guitar players, when they are sixteen, seventeen, eighteen years old, have a standard cultural activity, and it's a very fraternal thing. They drop acid and play rock and roll all night, which is a very lady-exclusive experience. So my experience was very solitary. I would sit in the Ash Grove and listen to Taj Mahal or go home and listen to Skip James records. I wasn't part of that rock and roll acid experience, therefore to learn time, to learn about time in your body, I think is harder for women. Women still aren't taught that total lack of restraint that boys are.

*Do you feel
you have to be sexy on stage?*

I think I am sexy. I dig being sexy. I am a very man-oriented woman. Besides my business thing, I happen to love men. I love experiencing the differences between men and women. I feel that being a part of what I do. The stage is a very flashy place. The point of being on stage is that you make a distinction between yourself and the audience. The audience needs to be turned on, and I definitely think you should be sexy on stage.

I think the performer has a responsibility in any case to be very different, to dress flashy, to be gracious, to be somehow larger than life. People need that. You should be gold on stage. You go to a club because you want something to hit you, something to flash you. The problem that I've found is that a lot of men at these clubs that I've been working at really react badly. I wear low-cut things, a lot of silver and a lot of jewelry, a lot of make-up and my hair down. I try to make the very, very most of what I look like, because I believe in it, it's my conviction. I've had some guys come on to me in a very rank way. It's OK because it's an idea that they're responding to. If they saw me sitting here in my orderly shoes with my hair in braids, they would probably not want to come on to me. It's the idea.

How do you handle it?

I ignore it. I've not gotten to the point yet where I can pour a pitcher of beer on some guy's head. I would not go to the point of being hurt by my own graciousness. If I had to do something about it, I would, but nobody so far has made it so totally unbearable for me. It teaches me. I do my shows and then I retreat to the privacy of

Are fans a problem?

Not at all, they're really nice, with the exception of the drunk guys who holler and shout. But that's cool. They just want to hang loose themselves, which is why I haven't turned around and slugged anybody. The fans are incredibly nice people. They are people for the most part who have heard the music and are very turned on by it, and the music has touched that thing in them. A lot of them end up being friends.

What do you think
it is in your music that touches people?

My music is drawn from several personal places, the personal feeling of the music itself, and my personal experience. My focus is on self-direction and on love. I am very romantic. I have to believe, especially now, that that's what's going to do it. My stage show tries to convey that. My music has brightness and romanticism and it can also make people cry, because I've connected to some feelings in me, and then I take them out and I try to expand them enough so that they will connect to the same feelings in other people.

More than once, people have come up to me and said, "I hear this song and it sounds like it's always been here, the music sounds like it's always been around." I think it is just because of the connection I've been working on, a connection to what's always been around. There is an eternal music, and I'm a vehicle. It's up to me to sort of open myself up and let it flow through my particular configuration which is why my music comes out different than somebody else's. It still says that thing.

I try to construct my life such that I meet nice people. And I am meeting nice people. But that's also because I go out and play in public. If you play in a club, nice people come in, and audiences really reflect the people they come in to see. For instance, people who would come to hear the Dillards are so nice. You'd have to be nice to dig the Dillards, and when I'm playing on the same show, they dig me. What it's actually all about is people, and I think that's why people pick up on my music.

How do you feel
about reviewers and critics?

They have their craft, I suppose. I'm a writer, so I like writers. I don't understand the field of criticism, but it doesn't offend me. There was one major review of my album in which there was so much that was completely off the wall to me that it was just foolish. If I took it seriously, I'd have an ulcer. I appreciate, although I don't understand, what one does to make that choice to become a critic. But I know that there's no way a critic can hit the nail on the head any more than anybody can. I assume it's all a matter of personal taste, but I really am not sure.

As far as criticism being harder on women, it doesn't seem to affect me too much. But as much as a woman is going to be affected by anything in the world, she is going to be affected by criticism. If a woman can't keep it together in the studio, if her stage show is below par, if she has to continually rely on her management for her direction, then if she gets a bad review, it's going to break her heart.

I think music is a lonely field. I think rock and roll is a very self-important, self-strutting, at-its-infancy business, and anything that is self-important and strutting and at its infancy is very much alone. My business is not rock and roll, it's music, so I would have to say that all the real musicians I know are very lonely people. I suppose it is that loneliness that makes up able to write our music.

Do you think
rock and roll is a lonely business?

My personal life is upside down right now. It's finally gotten to it, definitely. I'm not a person who believes that the outside world affects what the inside person does, but I'm in a period of transition right now. I'm expanding, it's forcing me to grow, very much so, and I'm outgrowing a lot of my former conditions and circumstances. I've been a lot of places in the last few months, and I'm going to be out on the road again. I've had to suddenly become so self-reliant. I have two suitcases and that's what I live out of.

My picture of what's important to me, of what kind of a home I want, how I want to spend my time, all that has been really turned upside down, definitely. I expect it to stabilize, but I don't think it will for some time. After you've been on the road for, say, two years, it becomes very difficult to settle down.

How does the
music business affect your personal life?

Oh yes. There is grace in a woman's home and in her love, in her children, in gardening, in cooking. There's no peace on earth like coming back into a clean house with fresh flowers and nice things. I believe in it very strongly.

I believe it's really biological. That may be paradoxical, because in some ways I'm one of the strongest and most independent of the lady musicians around. Perhaps it is because of my independence that I can look back on that other side of things and appreciate it. I don't think there's any greater satisfaction than really having a good man

Do you think about the traditional
American female role, kids, house?

and a good home and raising kids and just craving the nest. That's what we're about; but it has to come in its right time. That's what women have to learn. I couldn't do it now.

Do you think of yourself as a happy person?

Sure. I'm somewhat turbulent at this point in my life, but I'm happy because I do have a basic root connection to something in the universe. I'm a very strong believer in the self. There is a logic to what happens in our world, even the painful parts. I'm content to keep trying to enlighten myself. Unhappiness to me comes from unconsciousness.

Why do you think you are so strong, so independent?

I don't know. I have had certain benefits that perhaps some other people haven't had. I've been in analysis with an extraordinary man for some years. Maybe it gets down to something mystical. Maybe it's at the level at which, when I was young, I decided I was going to somehow figure out how to master my own fate, woman or not.

Has the women's movement made you aware of this?

I was married when I was eighteen. I don't know what the women's movement has done to me. I was already working on that stuff. I see it now more than I saw it then. What I see now is what is happening in women's music, and to me that's an extraordinary sign, and I really don't even know why. I can see what it's doing for a lot of other women, but I'm not a believer in movements, I don't trust them, because what they do is tend to distract you from the real business at hand, which is yourself.

A woman can say she doesn't want to wash the dishes anymore, but then she is going to turn around and the dishes won't be washed and it's going to drive her crazy, because he can't wash the dishes as well as she can, and she wants her house clean. Why does she want her house clean? Because she's a woman.

What the women's lib movement did for me I guess is make me aware. The focus is not on who washes the dishes, but on understanding who that woman is. I think that for the middle-stream housewives, it's really a vital thing. The resentment, though, the all-black and all-white stuff is nonsense. Men are not all clods. God didn't make the world such that men are all bad and women are all great. I happen to know some very great men, and some very great women also.

The point for a woman is to say, Who am I? Where do I fit in the universe? What am I put here to do? What's the best way I can do it? Is it a solo trip this time or am I supposed to have a man? If I'm supposed to have a man, then let me learn how to be both strong and submissive, to understand what my role is supposed to be, so I don't have to wind it up with all that insane resentment. There's a lot of pain in that.

The moment a new tune is finished, and I know it's good, and I'm loaded and it's three in the morning and I'm singing it to myself. The moment that the band finishes arranging it, and we've all been snorting coke and we're feeling hot and the damn thing sounds too good to be true, the arrangement is right and everyone's flashed. The moment that we're in the middle of it on stage and I can just feel the energy of the audience. It's a good piece of music and we get off stage and we know that the audience has understood what we were saying. And the moment that we finish recording it.

It's all the same thing. When the music is right and fresh, ha, that's it! That's really the feeling!

What do you like best about your work, what gives you the most pleasure?

EPILOGUE

Somewhere beyond all the words, there exists an obvious contradiction among rock and roll women. While not common to all, there are too many instances for it to be ignored. Stated simply, it is this: the life-style they are putting down is their own life-style; they often criticize each other for what they themselves do. For all their disdain, their distaste for the social scene and its frantic and self-conscious lack of even the most basic social amenities, rock women frequently live in the midst of it. Their insecurities prevent them from breaking out of the insulating world of rock and roll; thus they become preoccupied with pretense and image at the expense of personal evolution. They challenge a man's world on a man's terms, negating their greatest asset, their womanhood. They do not understand it and cannot use it to their own advantage.

In the end, it does not matter whom they know, what kinds of drugs they have taken, which men they have slept with, what kind of indiscriminate intellectualizing they have endured. What matters is their own sense of self—dignity if you will—and their ability to make both their personal and musical intentions clear.

ACKNOWLEDGMENTS

In light of the fact that efficiency just doesn't seem to be what it used to be, in almost all cases involving interviews in this book, contacting performers through managers and publicists was frustrating and often futile. When I called artists directly, however, there was rarely any problem.

Therefore, I am especially appreciative of those who did help, and I would like to thank Garry George and Joyce Giofu and especially Veronica Brice at Warner Bros. Records, Heidi Howell at Grunt Records, and Karen Shearer at MCA, for their help and cooperation.

Thanks also to Vince Romano and Richard Kung at Richard Photo Lab in Hollywood for their expert film development and speedy printing.

And special thanks to Marco Barla, without whom this book wouldn't be as coherant as it is.

DATE DUE

DEC 22 2004			